What are teens saying about the book?

"Taanvi created the most inspiring book for all teens that will uplift anyone who will read it. It is amazingly written and her story is so amusing and shows what a motivated person she is. She is always positive about everything and is determined to do what she loves. This will help anyone who is struggling with anything in life and is such a helpful book. An extremely powerful story of an incredibly smart young teen who always follows her dream and let's nothing stop her from doing what she loves. She absolutely nailed everything in her book!!"

Angelica Di Tillio

"Taanvi is such an inspiration for kids, teens, and even adults everywhere! Her book Uplift Teens Today, is a relatable and helpful source for any young person who feels alone, stressed, pressured or so many other feelings that come with the roller coaster that is life. As a teen myself, Taanvi's book gives open, positive, and realistic tools for managing intense emotions that teens encounter, and shares very helpful ways to be our own support system! She opens up by sharing her own life experiences and gives us her own successful coping skills for life. Taanvi has encouraged this generation to take the steps to better themselves, their minds, and their lives. Great job Taanvi! The world needs more amazing people like you!"

Kyleigh King

"Taanvi shares an important message in her book for teens, where she details the inspiring and intriguing journey of her move from Ireland to America. Her story not only connects with the hearts of young readers, but shows them how they can keep themselves positive and uplifted, even through the tough times in life. Taanvi is such an empowering role model. This is definitely a book for every reader."

Amy Zhao, Author & Entrepreneur

"In Uplift Teens Today, Taanvi shares her unique, yet relatable, struggles in life and how she managed them. It is so inspiring to hear tips and tools on how to manage your mental health from another teen! A must read for everyone!"

Sophia Pearson

1

"Uplift Teens Today is a useful book that I think a lot of people could relate to in today's world. The way Taanvi's writing is able to shift your thinking from negative to positive is outstanding. The positive outlook on life Taanvi shows through her writing, creates realistic ways that readers can change there own mindset. I think this book will be beneficial to anyone and everyone who reads it."

Aliya Sloan

"Taanvi's book, Uplift Teens, is truly an amazing asset for teenagers and beyond to empathize with her. Her book offers crucial strategies to manage the effects that come along with experiencing mental health battles. It is very well written in the way where I feel the emotions Taanvi is expressing throughout her journey and all the changes to America. I suggest others should make time to read her book, it may teach you a helpful thing or two!"

Anonymous

"This is a stunning book all about coping with change in this modern world. As a teen myself I know what it's like to suddenly have to go through numerous life changes all at once. This book I believe is relatable to multiple people's experiences and I wish I had this book when I went through them. Taanvi also gives wonderful, helpful, and insightful tips on ways to cope with those hard challenges and ways to overcome them. I recommend this book to all who are going through difficult changes in life."

Emmy H.

"There aren't many books about regular teen lives. Unbeknownst to most people being a teen is harder than it seems. Of course, we have all gone through it but everyone's story is different and their experiences vary. There was just something super relatable about Taanvi's struggles that makes the book easy to read and connect to. Taanvi has had a pretty hard teenage life since she moved to America but she has had a super positive attitude throughout it. Uplift Teens is a great book and I definitely recommend it!"

Lillian Farrell

"Very entertaining, keeps you hooked and shows the struggle of mental health... wonderfully done."

Sarika Sathyamurthy

"Taanvi's Book, Uplift Teens Today is a great book about changes through life and how to cope and deal with them, as well as showcasing how different it can be through different perspectives. In this book, Taanvi accurately represents hers and her family's move from somewhere she's grown up since childhood, to somewhere she's hardly ever heard of. Navigating through this difficult time, Taanvi shows how to make the best and how her view at this time in her book- as a kid, eager to embark on this new "adventure" could look like, rather her parents or their older friends and family, whereas their perspective might have been somber, nervous, and anticipation for this new chapter in their lives. This book highlights how important it is to stay true to yourself and your family, as well as the many things that are important to yourself, like family, religion, and interests. Taanvi symbolizes how changes can takeout a large toll on you but to always look for the bright areas and to keep persevering no matter where you are. Overall I believe this book describes a significant, important topic, told through the lenses of a young girl, and her family looking forward to her new home and this new era in their lives."

Anonymous

What are adults saying about this book?

"Self-awareness is a skill that not every adult has, and not only does 13-year old author and mental health advocate Taanvi Arekapudi possess it, but she is able to take that masterful skill and share it in a way that will make a deep impact on others. Uplift Teens Today shares tools that will help kids navigate challenging times in a way that is understood because it's also written from a peers perspective. Taanvi will leave an impression on your kids' heart because she so openly has shared hers. This book should be every kids companion. Kudos to Taanvi for her leadership, kindness and courage! "

Shari Alyse, America's Joy Magnet, Bestselling Author of Love Yourself Happy, 2x TEDx, TV Personality & Host

"A perspective we NEED to hear - some of the world's biggest topics such as the pandemic or immigration, but through the lens of the generation most affected by it. I have such deep respect for Taanvi taking her experiences and turning it into gems for her peers and all those who will read this book."

Daniel Ramamoorthy, 5x TEDx Speaker | Speaking Coach

"A trail of bright lightbulb moments through lived experience, Taanvi guides us with big heart, magic and motivation."

Ruth Fitzmaurice, Author of "I Found My Tribe"

"In sharing some of her challenging life experiences and how she has managed these, Taanvi has crafted a lovely story that includes skills we can all use to help us manage the painful emotions we'll inevitably encounter. Thank you Taanvi for being such an inspiration, and keep up the great work!"

Sheri Van Dijk, Psychotherapist, Author & International Speaker

"We have faced so many challenges recently that are out of our control. Young people especially have navigated uncertainties and impossibly challenging circumstances. In Uplift Teens Today, author Taanvi Arekapudi is a voice to her peers reaching out to let them know they aren't alone. Taanvi provides ideas and activities that help her readers stay positive when everything about life feels hard. But -- this is not just a list of inspiring activities! Taanvi frames her ideas within her own

challenging journey of moving across the ocean to a new home in America. As her readers also learn about her nearly two years (!) of online schooling during the pandemic, they discover how Taanvi used that time to build up a reserve of positive vibes so she could use them to uplift her peers. Readers will love to discover that her inspiring message comes to life thanks to the QR codes scattered throughout her book. Each QR code links to Taanvi addressing the reader as a dear friend that she is there to champion! If you are lucky enough to know Taanvi, you already know she uplifts people around her wherever her journey takes her. And -- if you are lucky enough to get a copy of Uplift Teens Today, you will be inspired to develop that same positivity and share it from within wherever your journey takes you!"

AmyLynn Schexnayder, Assistant Principal

"This is a fantastic book where Taanvi shares her own story as well as tools and tips to support young people's positive mental health and wellbeing. I feel that young people will find this book very relatable, helpful and supportive. It is beautiful written, engagingly, and informative. I highly recommend this book for all young people and especially those experiencing difficulties in their lives"

Louise Shanagher, Author, Mindfulness Teacher & Trainor Founder of Creative Mindfulness Kids

"Taanvi weaves a beautiful story that is also a master class in how to meet change and challenge in life! She authentically offers us tools to be more present, cope with anxiety, connect with ourselves and others, and dance with what life brings. Taanvi's experiences as a global citizen- and her "wise beyond her years" knowing- come together delightfully in this gem of a book, which is sure to inspire people of all ages to chillax and remember what matters!"

Peggy Fitzsimmons, Ph.D., Author of Release: Create a Clutter Free and Soul Driven Life.

"Every generation struggles with the world in which they are born. There is nothing new under the sun... THANKFULLY, the sun rises every day providing time for new opportunities.

How wonderful it is that Taanvi Arekapudi arose with helping others in her heart. Her book Uplift Teens Today is a breath of fresh air in a society ripped in political division and overloaded with the weight of grief, stress, and discourse. If you struggle with change and feel out of place, you may find Taanvi's stories relatable.

She crafted Uplift Teens Today to help you to think positively. I hope Taanvi's work will be conduit for you to find peace in your circumstances and shift gears.

Tomorrow is never certain, but always dependent on the actions we take today. As we reflect on the past, live in the moment and plan for the future, let us always value the urgency of now. Be your best self today. Ask yourself, "If you do not have time to do it right today, when are you going to have time to do it over?"

Seek wise counsel. Remember there is nothing new. Someone has walked a similar path before. Be willing to learn, be encouraged and even be warned by others. Listen, apply advice appropriately and step out to forge your own path.

Enjoy the read and your journey forward!"

Jesse D. Hayes IV, President, Red-Tailed Hawks Aviation Academy

"Taanvi the Author has hit the nail on the head with her tools and techniques to uplift our moods and see situations and recognize emotions and become the support for ourselves. Not only does she mention them in easy ways to implement but she has tried them all and gave us the best. Pick up this book "Uplift Teens Today", take a deep breath, and get ready to regain control of your life! Definitely, a book to read - and learn from one of the best. A message from a teen to another teens or adults."

Srimanju Katragadda, Author of bestselling book "Connect To Your Inner Guide"

"Taanvi's personal story of strength, resilience, gratitude, and mindfulness is an inspiring glimpse into a young person's journey through the ups and downs of middle school life during a pandemic. Her true and honest recounting of how these experiences felt and her practical tips for how she managed through the tough times and overcame challenges are relevant, helpful, and empowering. I am grateful for the opportunity to learn from Taanvi, as I plan to implement these practices in my own life."

Tiffany Rodriguez, Principal

"In Uplift Teens Today, Taanvi Arekapudi demonstrates the value of sharing our life challenges and emotional struggles openly and honestly. For this is what she does whilst bringing the reader through the ups and downs of her transition from living in Ireland to living in Seattle and importantly sharing the concrete tools she used to

navigate some rough waters. Taanvi delivers coping skills in an enjoyable easily digestible manner ensuring this book will be an asset for any family."

Patrika Mani, Bodywork and Energy Therapist

Uplift Teens Today: Coping strategies for mental health

Copyright @2022 BITS Publishers

ISBN: 979-8-9869096-0-8

BITS Publishers

October 2022

This book is not an alternative to medical advice from your doctor or other professional healthcare providers. If you have any specific questions about any medical matter, you should consult your doctor or other professional healthcare provider. If you think you may be suffering from any medical condition you should seek immediate medical attention. You should never delay seeking medical advice, disregard medical advice, or discontinue medical treatment because of information on this book.

FIRST TEEN TO TEEN MENTAL HEALTH BOOK

UPLIFT
Teens Today

COPING **STRATEGIES** FOR MENTAL HEALTH

TAANVI AREKAPUDI

BITS
Publisher

I dedicate this book to everyone with mental health challenges –

in other words, all of us.

Table Of Contents

Foreword

When Taanvi Asked me to write to forward for her first book, without hesitation I said yes. This isn't always the case for me. As a mental health advocate who has penned seven of his own books I understand the importance of the needed voices that come into the space and understanding the brevity of this work. She might only be 13, but Taanvi is definitely one of those voices that understands and has a boldness that is so rare.

I remember meeting Taanvi at a Youth Mental Health conference in the spring and one of the first things that she had mentioned to me was that she wanted to write a book helping her peers as she noticed the overwhelming struggles that they are dealing with mentally and emotionally I lit up with excitement and hearing her Express her heart to want to help in this way. Writing a book is never easy and being able to accomplish this feat before stepping foot into a high school Is something that we are the reader of this book should not overlook.

With Uplift Teens Today, Taanvi has given us something that I believe we can all call from in one Way or another. Whether it's parts of her story that talk about some of the challenges that she faced, or her parents faced or if it's those moments of uncertainty that come with moving around the world and having to embark upon new places and find yourself time and time again. I believe Uplift Teens today is a great reminder of our mental framing in tough times.

I know that it can be very easy for us to see very tough situations and experiences and our mind begins to race with over thinking and from that over thinking sometimes we can give power to negative thoughts that can turn into negative actions. What this book does is gives us some really good tools to help in moments like that. To help us to re-center in times of doubt or uncertainty and to be reminded that even in the toughest of times our troubles and traumas do not last always.

As you read through this book I want to encourage you to take your time to find your self, your voice and your ability to think positive and implement positive practices that will better help your mental health as you navigate life. I am so grateful to be working in this mental health field and to come across people like Taanvi who are the bold voices of our future and the reminder that we need that no matter where we are in life, no matter who we are and I'm at our age we are capable of creating things that will leave such an amazing impact on this world.

Richard L. Taylor Jr

Mental Health Expert | Speaker | Author

Preface

Dear Readers,

Ever since I was seven years old, I've always wanted to write books. I would write short stories and journal all the time. And after all this time, here I am, with this book, *Uplift Teens Today*, as a result of all the twists and turns my life took in the past few years. Just a few years ago, I used to live in Ireland and then everything changed when I moved here with my family. I had so many friends there, I loved my school, spent so much time with my family, and was really having the best time, never having gone through any big struggles. All this changed when my parents decided to move from Ireland to the US. At the beginning I was incredibly excited, but didn't know what it all meant until we started packing and were ready to make that move. The initial months of the move made me face so many new emotions in life, and I had no clue what I was going through. I couldn't talk to anyone because I didn't know that what I was going through was something that I needed help with.

Only when everything got piled up, and one day I just burst out crying, that my parents and sister realized I was going through these emotions but didn't let them out. I was so anxious, and my breathing became heavy. My parents and sister hugged me and reminded me about how important it is to share my emotions. My mom shared the quick meditation tip that we used to do in Ireland. This really helped me to calm down and from then on, whatever emotion I used to go through I shared it with them and then they helped with tools and techniques to adapt to change in a positive way.

This open conversation not only helped me but my friends too. This inspired me to start the Think Positive club in my school so that we could help more peers. As part of the club, we used to have open spaces for everyone to share and learn from each other. We also brought in guest speakers who would share their experience and tools and techniques to help us as part of our daily lives. This book is an accumulation of all those learnings and practical tips that have worked for me and for other peers. To further connect to you all, I have shared my own journey of life, highlighted the challenges I faced, and the tools that I used to help myself along the way. Look out for the lightbulbs, that's where the tools will be!

The tool that really helped me the most through this is the square breathing technique. This helped me calm down and ground myself. It's really simple and can be done anywhere at any time. For this tip, you imagine a square and follow along the sides. While imagining each of the sides labeled with 1, 2, 3, and 4. Along the first side, breathe in for four counts. Then, hold for four counts, breathe out for the next four, and finally, rest for the remaining four counts. And you can do as many rounds as you would like.

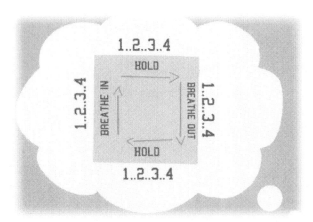

Through this book, my goal is to reach out to as many of you as possible, so you can pick tools and techniques that work for you and make them a routine in your daily life, share it with your friends, and spread the positive vibe around.

We all have tough times in life, and it's about how we bounce back from those experiences with new learnings. I hope the tools and techniques outlined in this book can help you in those moments. I would also like to acknowledge a deep gratitude to you for picking this book and helping break the mental health stigma through helping yourself and others. I hope you relate to my story as it's connected to all of us and know that you are not alone. We are all in this together and it will get better.

This book is for everyone - and that includes adults too. I have shared many family bonding tips that my family got to implement and practice and have seen change in our lives, as well as many individual tips and tools.

I hope you enjoy reading this and that it can help you in one way or another. You are not alone and you got this.

"Happiness can be found, even in the darkest of times, if one only remembers to turn on the light." — Dumbledore

Warmly,

Taanvi Arekapudi

P.S. Be the Best You, that You can Be!

Acknowledgment

This journey has been very challenging, it was complete roller coaster of emotions. There were days when I asked myself, if I will ever be able to complete this book. Every time I faced a challenge, it took lot of courage, motivation, and determination to come out of that and get started on the journey of writing the book. Only one thing that kept me going, was, the urge to ensure I share what I learned and benefited from during my difficult times to my peers to let them know **"You are not Alone"**.

I sincerely thank everyone who has helped me along this journey. I couldn't have done it without all your support. I would like to thank my parents for being with me every step of the way and for beng incredible role models, my grandparents for always encouraging me, my sister for whom I could not have written this book without, and my friends for supporting me throughout this. I would also like to thank a few amazing people who have been pivotal in this process; Lynn Colwell for taking the time to edit and help shape this book, Richard L. Taylor Jr. for mentoring me through this process, Shari Alyse for preparing me for the media, Barbie Collins Young for supporting me through the National Alliance on Mental Illness, Jesse D. Hayes IV for encouraging and supporting me through Red-Tailed Hawks Flying Club, Avery Mani Brooks for some of the wonderful drawings in this book, and Michele McLaughlin for supporting me through the KCLS Library.

Introduction

Let's start from the very beginning. My parents were born and raised in India, and they moved to Ireland for work in 1998. My sister was born in Ireland in 2006 and I came along in 2009. This story starts in Ireland, in my house, where I thought my whole life would be.

It was a regular weekend, and after getting up, we made breakfast and headed to the oval-shaped dining table where my dad was to one end, my mom to the other, and my sister and I beside each other. The weekend was my time to relax, and not think about all the homework and tests from school. It is when I can spend time with my family and just chillax.

Like any other weekend, we talked about school and friends, and enjoyed each other's company while eating our yummy Irish breakfast. The rich buttery taste from the bread still lingered on my tongue. This breakfast was our family favorite.

As we were all eating, my dad said he had an announcement. We were surprised and excited because we never really had "big announcements" like this. Usually, the big news would be going to India to meet our grandparents or going on a holiday somewhere in Europe.

My sister and I exchanged glances and were impatient to hear the news, and when we looked across to my mom, it looked like she was feeling the same as we were. We were sitting on the edge of our chairs.

"There is a new opportunity in my office for me, and it is a higher-level job," my dad said. My sister and I were so excited to celebrate and congratulate him because this was his dream. Then, not knowing that we had cut him off mid-sentence, he resumed, "That job is in Seattle so we may have to move there." We were so excited because to us it sounded just like a vacation! But, to be honest, we didn't understand what it meant, as we were thinking from our point of view, being nine- and eleven-year old's.

Later on in the week, when the topic came up again, my parents mentioned that we should go to Seattle for a trip so my dad could check out his office and team, and so that we could see the place and decide if we would like to move there or not. My sister and I were very excited about the trip, and we both were on top of the world. I was really looking forward to this trip, especially the long flight, and sleeping in a hotel room. We loved going on family vacations and we were as excited about this as any other family trip! As a family, during summer or school breaks we would explore countries in Europe. For instance, we traveled to Greece, Iceland, and other places. We all love adventures and traveling around the globe.

When we booked the tickets for the trip, my sister and I told our teachers that we would go to Seattle for two weeks. It was close to our mid-term break for Halloween. So, it was the perfect time to go on vacation and not miss a lot of school. I asked my teacher if he could give me homework for the few days I would miss over the trip, and he gave me Irish homework to learn and say different words to the people I would meet in the U.S. I was so excited that we could go to AMERICA, because in movies they show it as the "dream" country.

Halloween in Seattle

When we arrived in Seattle, Halloween was coming up. So, before our trip, we packed costumes that we had bought in Ireland. We stayed in Redmond, WA. close to my dad's office. The hotel was lovely with a kitchenette, a nice option we hadn't seen before. We made a plan that my dad would go to the office every day and when he returned in the evening, he would take us to movies, restaurants, to meet his old friends and go sightseeing.

On the morning of the 31st, my sister, mom and I were in the Redmond Town Center. There were not many people around - and no kids. Then we realized schools weren't off in Seattle for Halloween.

When my mom asked the shopkeeper about it, she said there was a huge trick or treat that happened from 4 p.m. and to come and see hundreds of children. She said that we were welcome to join. So, that evening as a family we walked to Redmond Town Center to celebrate Halloween together wearing our costumes. We walked around to many shops with the crowd of other kids, saying, "Trick or Treat." Halloween in Redmond was an awesome experience, and

my favorite part was when my family and I walked to every shop together.

After entering almost all the shops, we headed back to the hotel and opened up our bags filled with candy. I have to admit, I was pretty exhausted because it was a lot of walking in the cold. My facial muscles were also sore from all the smiling.

When my sister and I opened the bag, and dumped the candy onto the hotel bed, we saw so many varieties of candies like Hershey's, Swedish fish, Sour Patch, and many more. We never had so many kinds of candy in Ireland, so we wanted to taste the various candies and see which were our favorites. I knew this was probably the most enjoyable and special Halloween we had ever had.

I have to say, Halloween in America was an altogether special experience, although we still missed our normal tradition. Our normal tradition would be that my sister and I would go trick or treating with friends in my neighborhood. And in the night, all the families would gather together to see the fireworks.

Every day my dad would leave the hotel after breakfast and would go to work at his new job. That meant my sister, my mom, and I were at the hotel, so we made it entertaining. Some days we would walk around Redmond Town Center, then go to the French Bakery where we got delicious treats. Other days my sister and I would do drawing competitions to entertain ourselves. When walking around, we noticed the weather was like Ireland and we loved the adventure of the exploring.

Searching for Houses

On some days we looked at houses for sale. We noticed the houses we looked at were much bigger compared to Ireland because here there were multiple bedrooms, and in Ireland, my sister and I shared a bedroom. Our favorite part was walking into every house, and imagining our life in it. We would choose who was going to get which bedroom. On the other hand, my parents were thinking about the logistics behind each house, for instance seeing if there was an elementary school for me and a middle school for my sister close to the house.

When my mom searched for shrines in Seattle, there were so many. As a family, we go to shrines regularly, so we can pray to multiple gods, and we do pujas for big celebrations in Hinduism. We were delighted to see that there was a temple, which was nice for my family and me because in Ireland where we used to live there weren't any temples. We would fly to London every few months to visit them. We were all so grateful about this, so we decided to go to one of the temples and pray. We were pleased when we saw how big the temple was, and how energetic and powerful we felt after going inside.

My sister and I were thrilled about the big houses in America and the really big schools. Comparing them to Ireland, there was a big difference and it was nice to see how each house is structured in a unique way. Our favorite part was to imagine ourselves living in the houses for real.

Searching for Schools

After looking at so many houses, we came across an open house for a place in a newly built neighborhood. The house was close to both types of schools we were looking for. So, we first went into the middle school to check it out for my sister. When we walked into the building, we saw the office to the left. My parents told the secretary that we were thinking of enrolling my sister to this school. Then, in a kind and welcoming way the secretary showed us around the school and helped us learn more about it, and its programs. The school itself was much bigger than our school in Ireland and so were the other schools around the area.

Next, we went to the elementary school that was close by the house and the middle school. We talked to the people at the office and they showed us to my probable 4th-grade teacher. When I introduced myself, I said I was from Ireland, and he said he had some family connections in Ireland. It was so great to relate to my teacher about Ireland, and I felt somewhat safer knowing 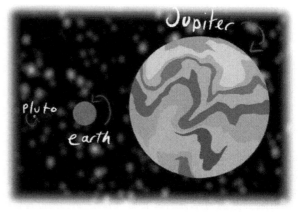 there was someone else from an Irish background. It felt good and relieving to be able to connect with him, especially as he could be my teacher. Because looking at the map comparing Ireland to America is like comparing Pluto and Jupiter.

We were both set on moving and were positive about it, as we were thinking moving would all be easy. Mostly what set the decision for me and my sister that we wanted to move was probably because we got really tempted by the big houses and broader education structure, so we basically judged the book by its cover. But my parents were still considering the pros and cons of moving. They were settling with the idea of applying for a visa and seeing what would happen next, and whether we would get the visa and move or not. My sister and I were confused because of all the legal processes to apply for a visa, and it was all way too complex for us to understand.

The two weeks packed with lots of plans, were over so fast. But, we all had a great time, and it was a very beautiful place. We returned to home to Ireland after a long flight, and continued with normal school routines.

Visa Process

At last, we got an interview for the visa. My parents were anxious because this was a significant step. After the interview, we patiently and eagerly waited to find out the decision on our visa and learn whether we would move or not. For the most part, we didn't tell our friends and teachers because we weren't sure whether we would get a visa.

After some time, we celebrated with our friends because we got the visa approval! We were so delighted and excited and my parents were very relieved. At this moment we knew that our lives would change - different schools, different friends, and different cultures. We were going to start our lives in another place, so we all stayed positive and hoped for the best. My family and I were joyful and thankful that my dad could join his new office.

In the midst of all this, we went to India as my cousin was having his Dhoti ceremony. This ceremony celebrates when young boys move into adulthood. They are symbolically honored with a Dhoti (Indian garment). We loved the time we spent with our cousins, aunts, uncles, and grandparents during the trip.

When we came back from that trip, we didn't have much time to sell the furniture, paint the house, and pack our moving boxes and luggage. My sister and I had six bunnies, and because we were moving, we had to give them away. It was very hard for us (especially my sister as she loves animals so much) to leave them with another family. I was very upset that we had to leave our bunnies, because they were really nice and showed me a new experience. When we first got them, I was scared at first, but then slowly with some help from my sister I started to enjoy their company. So, when we had to give them away, I felt like I was going to lose part of my happiness, and part of my family because we were so used to having them around.

I started to feel like I was losing things, and with losing the material objects I also thought I would lose the memories. For instance, when we were giving away our family bed couch, I was feeling sad, as I remembered so many memories where my family and I would all cuddle up and watch a movie. When we gave it to another family, I felt like I had to say goodbye and that it would never be mine again. But those times went by in a haze and there was a lot of things to do for my parents. My sister and I helped as much as we could, by packing boxes and cleaning the house for the new tenants.

Gratitude Jar

Even during the hectic times, we still carried on our "gratitude jar" tradition. We keep a gratitude jar and write on post-it notes about events we were grateful for and then we place them in the jar. At the end of the year, we open it and read them aloud, recollecting those memories. That time when we opened the notes at the ending of 2018, we all sat on my parents' bed. We began reading from the gratitude jar by sticking our hands in one at a time, and picking up a post-it note and reading it aloud remembering those times. Things we wrote included events that we were grateful for, like how we celebrated festivals together, or how we went to that nice restaurant together and the fun moment that happened. My sister and I were involved throughout the year with the tradition.

I love this tradition, because I feel like we get to relive moments and recollect such great memories. It also reminds me of all the things I did throughout the year. I also love to see how each one of us in my family is grateful for particular events. I love that some things I may have forgotten, I get reminded of by others in my family's gratitude notes, which helps me to recollect more memories from the year. This tradition brings my family closer, giving us more time to bond. Spending that time with my family opening and reading the notes really cheers me up and gets me in a great mood.

Gratitude Jar

A gratitude jar is a fun and great way for anyone to practice gratitude.

This is a **great** way to invite more **joy** and **abundance** into anyone's life through the **power** of **gratitude**. Doing it with your **family** makes it even more **special**!

Step 1
Write down the things and events you're grateful for on pieces of paper.

Step 2
Put all the pieces of paper in a jar.

Step 3
Open the jar, with your family once a year, may it be Thanksgiving or a time that you set as a family for tradition.

Goodbyes

Those times were all so rushed. It was Christmas break which also meant we couldn't say a proper goodbye to everyone, mainly, our really good school friends that we spent our whole life with. I didn't know when saying goodbye, how long would it be until I met my friends again. My parents said maybe three years.

I have this awesome and great friend; her name is Angelica and we were BFFs since a young age. It was hardest for me to say goodbye to her. In school, we always spent our yard time (recess) creating new games and playing them. We would try to beat each other on who could finish the assignment faster in class. We would have playdates every Friday making slime, and doing arts and crafts and we would create "potions" by pouring water and placing leaves into a bottle. It sounds weird, but trust me, we had lots of great times together. She and I were always in the same class because the students in the class are the same every school year, but the teacher would change yearly. This was the norm in primary schools in Ireland; it helped to build stronger friendships, as we got to see each other often.

I had hinted to my bestie about why we were going to Seattle before our trip. After all, I couldn't keep it in, even though I knew it was just a trip to check out the place.

After our trip, Angelica's family invited us over for a goodbye dinner after we shared the news that we were moving to America. They were heading to Italy for Christmas, and I wouldn't be seeing them the last week of school before our final move.

I was looking forward to this dinner, so I made this game for her and her younger brother out of paper and it was lots of fun to play together. Angelica's family are

Italian, and they made pizza for dinner. All the pizzas looked so unique and different, very unlike Pizza Hut. But the instant me and my family took a bite, we went on and on giving compliments about the delicious pizza. It was the best homemade pizza we had ever had!

Then, we all got pretty emotional when taking our last pictures together. This was the part where we both started to frown, and tears started uncontrollably rolling down our cheeks. We both knew we would miss each other so much. And we knew it was going to be hard to keep our connection. I was afraid that I would get replaced by the other friends she already had and that I would have to start from scratch making friends. I was so worried that I would miss my best friend and I wondered whether when I came back to visit, would we still be this close and this tight.

That thought made me uncomfortable. So, with both families sitting in the living room, we started to think of ways we could stay connected and decided to FaceTime each other every week even with the time difference and to write letters. This made it a little easier to say goodbye, but we were still going to miss each other like crazy. We were hoping to meet very soon again. Those last couple days,

31

we both stayed in tight connection, and made cards for each other, wrote poems and made broken heart necklaces. We would each wear a side to remember our friendship.

Leaving behind my friends, school, and house I grew up in was really hard. I knew things wouldn't be the same again, but I didn't really know how different they would be. When we were in the airport, I felt kind of lost. I was moving to this unknown place, and I didn't know how long it will be till I visited Ireland. I felt like I was a nobody because no one would know me.

I observed my parents and sister. They were acting differently. It seemed like they also felt like it was going to be a big change. I tried to forget that emotion, and cheer my family up, but I still felt it. I thought maybe this is what change feels like? I didn't like the sound of "starting over" because it sounded so dramatic, like you would have to do everything over again with a fresh start. But I started to understand what it meant, and now I realize that it is saying nobody knows you, and you get to make a new impression, have a new house, and go to a new school. I had an opportunity to create something new.

Now looking back it was start of emotions and deeper feelings I was having and carrying with me. We never know what events ahead will create a memory for lifetime and in which way.

Living in Seattle

We were on the flight to live in Seattle before we knew it. Once we landed, we took a rental car and drove to the hotel. My parents told us that this was the hotel we would stay in for a couple weeks till we got the house. So, we all took a rest for a couple days from the tiring and hectic last couple weeks.

In the hotel, it felt like I was still living in Ireland, because I brought basically everything with me on the flight to have in my new house. But, most importantly, I brought my calendar along with me. It's probably one of my most used items. I use it every night, by writing in three to four things I did that day. In the first place, I started doing this because my mom always has a calendar where she writes important events and the classes she has. I loved the idea so much that I really wanted to try it. At the beginning, I wasn't sure

I would use the calendar very much because I had a history of making and buying notebooks but not using them. I didn't want history to repeat, so I did it every day last year. Some days I was extremely tired so I postponed it by one day. I successfully completed that year's calendar by filling in every day, even though some of the days I had more than four, or less than three events. But all in all, I still achieved my goal.

Filling in my daily planner made me enjoy spending the time to reflect on my day and writing down my favorite parts. It was a great way to end my day on a high note. I also love that I can always look back and see what I did in that year. To recollect my day and write down my top few best events that occurred made my days much more enjoyable. I was so proud of myself for achieving that big goal, and was impressed with the first "notebook" I ever completed. I was so happy that I was very determined to continue this habit by filling in the next year's calendar, for 2019. So, in my suitcase with all my other things, was my new calendar. I hoped to continue this new tradition and fill in the whole calendar, especially because it was my first year in America.

Daily planner

Using a daily planner is a great way to cherish memories, and to remember them forever.

This is a **great** way to invite more **joy** and **abundance** into anyone's life through the **power** of **gratitude**. Doing it with your **family** makes it even more **special**!

Step 1
Write down memories in a diary every night. Key things that you were happy about, that happened that day.

Step 2
Repeat the same every night or a time that you choose as your tradition.

Step 3
When with the family or on holidays or when you are low, you can always go back and review the memories which will bring a smile to your face making you happy.

I realized when we write our good memories, we remember them for a long time. Generally, our brain is good to remember unpleasant ones easily. No extra effort is needed there.

Soon enough my sister and I had our first day of school in America, we joined the school midterm that means half-way through the curriculum, and we weren't sure what was being taught in the previous term. It was hard to go to a new school because the school culture was different, and I didn't have any friends, while everyone else in the class already had close friends. The hardest part for me was being in a new school without my sister. In Ireland, we had multiple grades in the same school, which was called primary school. So, my sister and I were in the same school, which meant we were always right there for each other during school and recess. And we had all our nursery school friends in the same school. It was a very familiar place for me because I had gotten used to it.

My sister mentioned that there was a volunteering club at her school called National Junior Honor Society, and that she could come into my elementary school and volunteer after her school ended (which was earlier than mine). I was looking forward to when she would start doing this so we could spend more time together, and I would feel less lonely at school. She said she would talk to the really kind librarian who is the advisor, and ask if she could start a little later in the school year.

In America, everyone in class and during recess when we would play in the playground noticed my accent and the way I used different words for things. Like we would say "estate" for "neighborhood." We would say "trolley" for "shopping cart" and "yard time" for "recess". Another big difference was with how we addressed our teachers. At school in Ireland when we would refer to our teacher, we would call them by their first name, and in the U.S., we call them by Mr., Mrs.,

Ms., followed by their last name. In school, I felt like there was more structured subjects, which was really overwhelming, especially because everyone else knew what they were doing, and how to use everything. I kept having to ask a lot of questions and I felt very confused. Without friends, and trying to talk to people and make friends, I felt lost. In a sense, I had no one to be with. I wasn't sure about many things, and things that were obvious to others weren't to me, which made me feel like the odd one out. In the classroom, I observed that the culture was different, because it was more individual compared to Ireland, where we would all analyze a text and write a summary together, raising our hands and talking with the teacher. The studies syllabus was different too. In Ireland we would work on our handwriting skills, and learn the Irish language. When I was starting off in my new elementary in the U.S., my teacher taught me the different American currencies and how to count coins. Learning this helped me when doing math word problems, and when we were in the hotel counting the money for laundry machines.

Jealousy

My dad was busy settling into his new work and getting everything set, and my sister was in middle school, which gave her lots and lots of homework. So, every day after school my dad would sit with her and help her with English and math.

Slowly, I started to feel left out, and didn't get much attention from my dad. This was because being in elementary school, I didn't have much homework, and I didn't understand how easy things were for me in school. While my dad was helping my sister, I spent time with my mom doing art and cooking.

I had this weird feeling every time I would go to class. It felt like there were butterflies in my stomach and I couldn't control the uncomfortableness. I also wasn't able to fall asleep at night; I was worried about school the next day and who I would play with at recess as I had no friends yet. I was scared to sleep on my own, because my sister and I had always slept together. Now I had my own room, sleeping all by myself. I also felt lonely, because my sister didn't play that much with me anymore. She was always busy with school work. I felt sad because I missed Ireland. I felt that my sister got more attention and I was always anxious about school. I was also really upset about missing my friends in Ireland and worried I wouldn't be in their thoughts, and that others would replace me and my friends and would forget about me. Suddenly, one day, when I was with my family I couldn't contain all these thoughts, and I burst out crying. Unexpectedly, this helped me to release all the inner talk.

We had a family discussion to talk about what was going on and why I had so many emotions I didn't share before. The discussion helped me to understand that my sister was struggling with her work and my dad helped her with it to make it easier for her as she had missed the first semester and had a lot to catch up with. The format in middle school was different than when she was in primary school in Ireland. The transition she was going through was challenging for her - getting to know teachers, what classes she needed to go to next, and making friends. I realized I could have been more understanding because this was new for her. We talked about being more empathetic of each other. She did want to spend time with me, but she had to get used to the new schedule and lifestyle she was experiencing. And so did all of us. It was the biggest change we had experienced as a family.

I also shared about how I felt like there was something different after coming here because in Ireland, I never really heard of the strong words like being anxious or depressed. But when I came to America, I heard these words being used by my classmates regularly. So, I started to believe I was going through these feelings too. It was a struggle for me to get all this negativity out of my head. I knew that I was having a tough time settling into a new environment and a new group of people, and especially a new home, and making friends in the neighborhood. It was hard to adjust, and create a new lifestyle and new routines. It all felt stressful and so different from Ireland. These thoughts were all causing me to feel more stressed, so I tried not to think about them. I knew I was feeling homesick and overwhelmed. Sharing this with my family helped me, but I did know that this feeling wouldn't just suddenly disappear. And, I was confused and unsure how to control these thoughts. My emotions were making me feel more negative and upset and I couldn't stay centered and calm. I always overthought things.

Sharing feelings & emotions

When a feeling or emotion surfaces, and you just want it to disappear and go away, it's best sometimes to express it. There are many ways to do this, and for each person it's different.

Explore many ways and keep track of what works for you.

Way 1
Tell it to someone you feel comfortable with and who you trust, like your parents, siblings, other family members, counselors, friends, etc.

Way 2
Express it in a creative form, like painting, bullet journaling, writing it down, or any other way that you enjoy and that lets the emotion out while also understanding it.

Way 3
If you enjoy sports, try listening to the thoughts and then letting them flow while doing whatever sports you enjoy – karate, basketball, tennis, running, soccer, etc.

Overwhelmed

My mom said she could do some meditation with us and that this might help all of us feel less overwhelmed and more grounded. It had been a while since we sat down and intentionally spent down time, and I was looking forward to seeing if this would help me. I was so excited to try it out, and asked if we could start right away. So, my mom started to guide us through a five-minute meditation session.

She waited until we were all in a comfy position, and we all closed our eyes and started to follow along. She guided us through some deep breathing, and in our minds transported us to a cloud. She told us to think about how we felt on the cloud, asked what belongings we brought. We slowly transitioned into a body scan breathing deeply into each of our body parts and the five minutes were over quickly.

It felt really good and helped me to feel calmer and concentrate on my breathing. I felt so relaxed, and I was able to shift my attention and thought to the meditation. I love when my mom guides me through meditations. I recollected when we were in Ireland my mom would guide us through meditation in an after-school club she hosted talking about mindfulness meditation and the different ways to practice it. It was nice to have her do it after so long, I felt so good when she transported me to a whole new world on a cloud and took me on a mind journey to a different place.

After that night, the weeks went by, and the same challenges returned. I was still anxious and overwhelmed by everything in school and at home. When I felt uneasy and agitated, I remembered that I was able to clear my thoughts and focus on breathing and let all the other thoughts fade, just like the night when my mom did meditation with my family and me. I wanted to recreate the feeling of being calm and grounded, because this would make it easier for me to be more focused and in the present moment.

So, one day during recess, I wasn't doing anything except overthinking things and I just thought why not try to create the calm and serene feeling I had when doing the mindfulness. I thought if I took a quick two minutes to pause and focused on my deep breathing - in, holding the breath and letting the breath out, that it would bring me the same feeling. While I was doing this, I slowly felt I was getting calmer and I was able to shift my attention and it made me feel better.

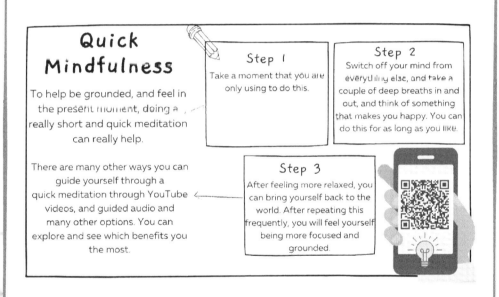

Quick Mindfulness

To help be grounded, and feel in the present moment, doing a really short and quick meditation can really help.

There are many other ways you can guide yourself through a quick meditation through YouTube videos, and guided audio and many other options. You can explore and see which benefits you the most.

Step 1
Take a moment that you are only using to do this.

Step 2
Switch off your mind from everything else, and take a couple of deep breaths in and out, and think of something that makes you happy. You can do this for as long as you like.

Step 3
After feeling more relaxed, you can bring yourself back to the world. After repeating this frequently, you will feel yourself being more focused and grounded.

By shifting my attention to whatever I chose, I tried to focus on identifying a word to put to the feeling I had. When I was doing this, I started to hear thoughts that were going on in my mind. These thoughts remained and didn't fade away, clearing my mind. The thoughts that were in my mind, were about school assignments, and how I was going to get graded on a big project. By being so calm and centered, I was able to pinpoint what I felt in the moment. I felt nervousness because of how restless I was when these thoughts were in my mind. After identifying the emotion, I was going through, I tried to acknowledge my feeling by addressing it. I did this by repeating a positive statement in my head like "I've got this," "I worked very hard on that assignment," "I am awesome and smart," and "I can do it," to make the negative nervousness fade away. After doing this, I observed that it helped decrease the feeling of nervousness and the thoughts about school. I felt more grounded and was able to feel myself in the present moment.

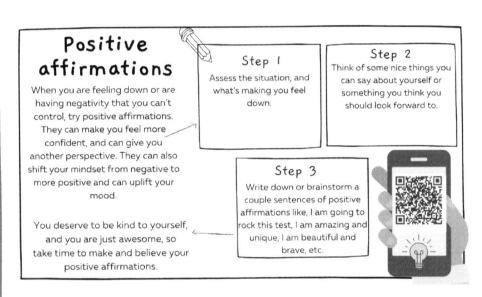

Positive affirmations

When you are feeling down or are having negativity that you can't control, try positive affirmations. They can make you feel more confident, and can give you another perspective. They can also shift your mindset from negative to more positive and can uplift your mood.

You deserve to be kind to yourself, and you are just awesome, so take time to make and believe your positive affirmations.

Step 1
Assess the situation, and what's making you feel down.

Step 2
Think of some nice things you can say about yourself or something you think you should look forward to.

Step 3
Write down or brainstorm a couple sentences of positive affirmations like, I am going to rock this test, I am amazing and unique, I am beautiful and brave, etc.

After that day, I tried repeating this process a couple more times. When I felt lonely, I would address this emotion by trying to start a conversation, which made me feel more social and connected with others. When I identified myself feeling anxious for an exam, I would talk to my family about this to help bring myself back to being calm and grounded.

Science Fair

On Monday, at my school assembly, my principal announced that we would be having a science fair and that everyone who wanted could participate, but 5th graders were required. As soon as the principal made that announcement and shared other events, my mind was wondering what the science fair was. Thankfully my teacher later in class explained what it was. He said that it was where you pick a hypothesis and make an investigation to prove it right or wrong. He said if anyone wanted to do it they had to sign up to get a tri-fold board, but he could help with ideas. The teacher gave the people who wanted to participate ten minutes during class to brainstorm ideas. I saw my classmates thinking and searching up different options online. The teacher shared pictures from last year's science fair and they looked cool. There were so many different questions, for example, can plants grow in different types of water temperatures? Does music affect our emotions? And so many more that I found really interesting.

I really like getting choice projects because I feel like I can share my creativity and my interests. But, it's hard to pick a project when there are so many options; and since I wasn't sure about the whole process, it made it even harder to decide which project would be the most interesting. After school, when I got home, I told my sister and my dad, and my mom about this, and they seemed really excited and very intrigued to hear my project ideas. I gave out a couple of ideas and they all had some connection with technology because I love gadgets and they interest me a lot. They really liked my ideas and I shared a couple of others ones that I could think of. My sister added and shared one about Virtual Reality, and I was curious to see what hypothesis I could make out of it. I was really intrigued by this and wanted to decide on something and get to work.

When I researched more about VR to get a better understanding so I could create a better hypothesis, I was curious about it, because it was like you could see a whole other world just by wearing a type of electronic goggles.

That got me thinking of questions I could ask like maybe, does keeping it on too much affect the brain? Does having the VR goggles for too long affect your eyesight? Is virtual reality bad or good for one's body? And others. I told my parents about this and asked my sister, which one sounded the most interesting. And she said, maybe think of something health-related because she knows I am interested in health. More specifically, she mentioned a health-related question like, how does it affect your eyesight? Because I know a lot of people want to know that, like, specific information instead of health, like a broad topic. Eyesight seems like a pretty good question. So, I was researching that online and I found a lot of debates about it. Some claimed it's good for your eyesight, but having it on too long is bad, and then some said it's really bad for your eyesight to have it on at all.

Since there are lots of controversies, I thought this could be a great topic because I could pick a side and talk a lot more about that and give reasoning to support my hypothesis. I was researching more about the side that said too much VR is bad for you because I wanted to know how much is too much. But when I was looking more about it, I was wondering what the experience would be like to have one. I thought of maybe making a 3D one where people can use it and feel the experience during the science fair. When I looked online for DIY ideas, I found this really cool images out of cardboard and watched a video, and I got a bunch of cardboard, got some tools and just got to it. I cut out different shapes, stuck them together, and then made a slip for the phone and downloaded some VR game apps. I made some little tweaks and painted it. When I tried it, it was awesome to experience the game like you were right there. This really inspired me to get started on my evidence and I was eager to learn more. Every day I went to school, I was just waiting for school to be over so I could work more on my project. After creating the model, I thought I would get started researching the history of it so I could provide more understanding. I also wanted to learn who created VR and learned about how it was invented. When the day of the science fair approached, I was feeling nervous because I worked so hard and I was afraid people wouldn't come up to my board because it was "too boring." After setting up my board, and putting my VR beside it, as I was waiting for kids to arrive, I wasn't sure if my stall was as cool and interesting as all the others. Finally, after what felt like hours of waiting, kids and families showed up and slowly looked at all the stalls. Then, finally at last, some kids came to my stall and wanted to try on the VR goggles, and I felt super-duper happy, and so relieved. After one person tried them on, slowly all the kids lined up at my board for a turn at playing a game through them. I was thrilled that the kids and families enjoyed the VR experience, and it made me so happy to know I was able to pull off such a big project.

After my dad was off the phone with my grandparents one day, he told my sister and I that they would be coming to the US in less than a month, and they would be staying for six months. My sister and I were delighted because we missed them so much, and we wanted to show them everything. We planned on going cherry picking, playing games, and spending quality time with them. We were so happy and were looking forward to show them everything, and to talk with them. We were counting down the days and were so excited to collect them from the airport.

Family Notes

The weeks were going by pretty fast, and in school there were many tests and quizzes coming up for me and my sister. It felt like we weren't able to talk about how we were feeling, prepared or not, and we weren't able to take time and just say good luck enjoy the test because sometimes when I was ready to talk, she was busy. So, I decided to leave a note writing "I love you so much Akka, you are going to rock this math test and I hope you enjoy it! :)". I was thinking of the best place to hide it in so it could be a surprise. So I thought if I put it in her pencil case when she goes to school and takes out her pencil case for her math test, she would see the note.

That day when she came home, before saying anything about her math test, she gave me a big hug and said "Thank you for the note, Taanvi." I was delighted that she liked it. Just like that, we began to write good luck notes to wish each other luck for tests, as we knew how much the other studied.

My mom and dad started writing notes to us too, and we did for them. As a family we all started to write love you notes to each other because we saw the impact the receiver and sender got from the notes. After writing the note, we hid it somewhere the receiver went regularly so it was a surprise for them.

I love writing the notes because I feel excited to let the other person know I love them and am so thankful for them in my life. I also love receiving the notes because they fill me with so much joy and make me feel special and valued. After a while we wrote these notes more regularly for different reasons like saying "Good Luck," "I Love You," "You are the Best," "Thank You" and others. We loved sharing our love through notes. It was a creative way to share our love and gratitude. It helped me to show more thankfulness towards my family for being so awesome and to encourage them, too. It is a great way to communicate, and because it's unexpected the notes have so much value. It is interesting for me to see the impact I feel when receiving a small note. it brings me joy and happiness.

Writing notes

Writing notes is a great way to share kindness and appreciation with others.

This can also create a chain, if the person who got the note gives one to someone else making them feel appreciated as well.

Step 1

Write a note to a person about something you appreciate in them.

Step 2

Keep the note in a secret place they go to daily.

Step 3

Feel the joy of giving a note to someone.

Anxious

School started to get more challenging, especially because of a big exam coming up called the SBAC. In Ireland we used to have big exams like this, but they were pretty simple multiple-choice questions in a printed paper booklet. My teacher said that this SBAC testing is online, takes an average of two hours to finish, and that the results go into my record. After hearing this, I was really anxious about it, especially knowing it would go into my record, and is a way to track my growth in school. I wanted to do really well, but wasn't sure how it would work or the type of questions that would be on the exam. My teacher said we would take it in two and a half weeks.

That day during recess, I heard my classmates talk about how they were going to bring coffee to keep them energized, and would also bring gum and snacks to keep them awake. I wasn't sure if the test would be so hard that they need all this, or if they were exaggerating. I started to feel a little panicked because if they needed caffeine and coffee, I thought I would need that too and I never had coffee so I was really confused. I decided to bring a little bit of candy that day and see if anyone else was eating, and if they were for fun, I would too.

I wanted to prepare for the SBAC exam daily, by brushing up everything I knew so I could get a good score, accurately representing my knowledge. So, when I got home after school, right after I finished my homework, I took time to learn more advanced material, and also spend time remembering more of what I learned before in math and English. I worked hard learning new content, and also trying to remember topics covered in the past. I made studying for the SBAC a part of my schedule. I realized that I was rushing my homework just to prepare for the test and I started to feel stressed out. There were a lot of assignment due dates coming up, from English to history essays. There were a lot of things circulating in my head. After school that Friday, when I walked home with my sister, I felt overheated and extremely tired. But when we got home, I still studied and worked hard with new concepts so I would be prepared for the test.

The next week went by normally. I continued to study for the test and do homework. I was preparing for all sorts of things that might be on the test, and sometimes even got a little annoyed when I forgot the basics and had to work on remembering them.

The final week before the SBAC came up quickly, I felt very unprepared, even knowing how hard I had studied. Usually, on tests where I get graded, I get pretty good marks that satisfy me. Keeping in mind that this exam was different than usual tests because it was to check our overall knowledge, made me feel nervous and unsure. When I came home from school Monday, my family asked why I was acting differently. I told them that the exam was making me really nervous and I wanted to learn lots of material, but also concentrate on school assignments, and wasn't sure which I should prioritize.

When I finished talking, and was waiting for a response from my parents, it started getting harder to breathe, and then it felt like I wasn't able to catch my breath. It began to hurt when I tried to take in deep breaths. I was having some heavy breathing issues and a tight chest. My sister, my mom and my dad were all concerned and weren't sure what was happening to me. After a couple of long seconds, the pain went away and I was able to freely breathe again. My family was concerned for me and told me that I might be putting too much pressure on myself and that I should relax. But, when they were saying this, my mind was thinking of how scary and hard what happened was, and as that was the first time it ever happened, I was wishing for it not to happen again.

My parents suggested that while working, I could try to take breaks, which might help me to get more work done while still being focused and grounded. Taking their words into consideration, I told them I would try taking a five-minute break when working and observe if it was beneficial.

I was curious to see if this would help me, and really wanted to do anything that would help to not have the breathing pain repeat. So, I tried it that evening when I was doing my homework. It felt unusual to study and then leave the computer for five minutes to stretch and move, but when I came back from the short break, I noticed that I was more focused. Taking that break helped me to bring a fresh mind to my studying.

I did this for the rest of the week until the day of the test, and I was so thankful I didn't have more breathing pain. I was so glad that taking a small break helped me calm down and feel less stressed out. On test day, I felt more relaxed, and knew that I would try my best and be happy with the results. So, I persisted and at the end of those tiring two hours, glued to the computer clicking answers, I was able to relax with the relief that I had taken the SBAC.

When I tried taking breaks after the SBAC exam for my regular homework, I enjoyed it and was actually excited for those brain breaks and worked hard until they came up. During brain breaks, I would spend time with my mom doing art work or watching tv.

I would also go biking with my sister if she was free. Sometimes I would play games with my dad, basically anything that would give me a rest from working. I noticed after doing this for a while that I was starting to be more focused, and while working I had a smile on my face. During these breaks I love to spend time with my family, and do the other things that make me happy and feel good.

Brain breaks

Taking a break when working on something that makes you feel overwhelmed or stressed can be a great way to help to calm and return more focused.

This is really beneficial when doing homework, projects or even preparing for a test.

Step 1
Decide when the time is right to take a quick break, and how long it will be.

Step 2
Take the break, and try leaving behind all your thoughts and switch off.

Step 3
When you feel more centered, you can return and try to push through until your next break.

It was finally time to collect our grandparents from the airport, we were so excited. Before we went to the airport, we created a" Welcome Home Nani (grandma) and Thatha (grandpa)!" sign. Then we made our way to the airport to collect them. As soon as we saw them, we were delighted and our faces were stuck smiling the whole time in the car ride home. We talked about the things we wanted to do with them. We were psyched to see them, and tried to give them the biggest welcome possible.

The first couple days we let them rest after the long flight, and after that we played after school, and talked about our day. We loved talking to them, and it felt so good to spend time with them. They talked about how things were going in their apartment in India. My grandma showed my sister and I how to make Muggulu which are thought to bring prosperity to homes. We both practiced and learned from my grandma, who does it daily. Our grandpa and grandma also taught us Telugu poems and taught us how to recite them. It was great to spend time with them because they made it so entertaining with different activities, and gave us unconditional love. While our grandparents were settling in, it gave us such a thrill to think of all the fun things we had to look forward to during their visit. It also gave us a nice distraction from all the overwhelming aspects of the beginning the school year.

The next week, our dad said there was a "Bring your kid(s) to work day" on Friday. My sister and I were so psyched for it because we had wanted to see our dad's new office. My dad said that there would be a make your own ice cream event, photo shoots and much more. My sister and I were looking forward to Friday to see where my dad works every day and the cafeteria he talks about so much. I was just waiting for the week to be over so we could go and enjoy.

On Friday, I had a fractions and decimals math test, and I thought I did pretty well. After that, I was counting down the hours until school ended and we could go to his office. When school was finally out for the week, my sister and I walked home. When we reached the house, we quickly grabbed a snack and hopped in the car waiting for our dad to get the car started. He had a day off work that day, but still wanted to bring us to his workplace. It was so cool to make ice cream at the event, and the ice-cream was really yummy and I was just amazed by the process. When we had food in the cafeteria, we got Mexican food. We also got some donuts from the food trucks that were outside. The long line for the donuts truck was definitely worth the wait.

We saved some donuts for my mom, so when we got home, we gave some to her because she loves donuts. The event was so awesome, and was a really nice experience because we got to see so many different jobs. And, to see our dad's work and work life made me feel really special. It was also really lovely to see all the stalls set up around the building, and going around it with my dad and sister was the best part because it was so relaxing and interesting to see another part of my dad's personality in his office setting. We had heard so much about it, but having the opportunity to actually get to see the office made such a difference. In Ireland we used to visit Dad's office during vacation time, and that was super exciting, so being able to have that same experience here, was really special.

School Project

After that exam, during history class, I was really looking forward to learning more about the Oregon Trail and reading more about life in the mid-1800's as that's where we left off. As a class, we had just finished reading our last textbook about the Oregon Trail, and my teacher announced that we would work on a presentation for a couple of weeks to share what we learned.

I was so excited because I felt like I knew everything that there is to know about the trail, and thought the assignment would be simple. When my teacher handed out the grading rubrics to everyone in class, as I was scanning through the paper, I noticed that there were a lot of requirements for the slideshow we had to create, as well as confusing questions that I didn't understand. I knew it was going to be a lot of work and a whole lot of effort as I wanted to get "exceeding standard" in the assignment, and put that as my goal. Knowing that it would take some hard work and focus I decided to try my best. The teacher said that we would start on the presentations soon. My mind was circling through many thoughts - excitement about the project and uncertainty about the difficulty.

The teacher instructed us on how to set our project. Following along, I opened a new blank presentation and started off by typing the questions. When I completed typing the questions, and was supposed to type the answers to the questions, I wasn't able to find any of the information to answer them. I was really confused because I had read the textbook and it seemed like everyone else in class was typing away with their answers. I didn't feel like reading anything to find the information because I was tired and felt like I couldn't do anything and just wanted to give up. When I got home after that exhausting day, I felt I had wasted a whole hour during history staring at the computer without typing anything. Or reading anything because I knew it would be boring to re-read it.

I told my sister what I felt, and that I couldn't find motivation to do the assignment. When I talked with her, I suddenly felt the tight chest, and breathing pain and it was really hurting. My sister was really confused, and called my parents to come up and they came and helped me to calm down.

My parents discussed bringing me to the doctors to check if everything was ok. And scheduled an appointment for the next week. In the meantime, my sister suggested, "Because you are feeling overwhelmed, maybe you could do something to distract yourself so when you return to work on it tomorrow, you can focus with more concentration?" I agreed with her, and thought I should take my mind off it. To do this, I decided that I should do the thing I enjoy most. So I asked my mom, dad and sister if they wanted me to make them something out of cardboard. My sister said she would like me to make her a bookshelf for the books she brought from Ireland. I was so excited that I started right that moment. In about two hours, I had it ready in her room, and started to put her books in to surprise her. I felt more relaxed after doing something creative because all my focus was on that, and my thoughts were not distracting me. When doing this I came across the book "Diary of a Wimpy Kid: The Long Haul" and flipped to a random page. When I started to read and look at the images, Greg (the main character) was saying how he was excited for summer vacation, and was looking forward to school ending so he could spend time doing whatever he wanted.

This made me think of how long it was until summer, and I realized there was only one month till summer vacation. I was really pumped, and was so happy that I wouldn't have to do any assignments during the summer. I realized that the Oregon trail assignment would probably be my last one in 4th grade. I was delighted and told my family about the great realization I had.

Looking Forward

When you need motivation to do something like a school project or reach a goal, this tip may help you to feel motivated by looking forward to something that may be happening in the near future.

This is one of the ways you can try to get motivated, and it can be really helpful if you sometimes need a push.

Step 1
Understand what motivation you need, and for what task.

Step 2
Think about the events that are coming up soon that you may look forward to, like maybe the summer, meeting friends, a trip, new computer, school breaks, etc..

Step 3
Try to look forward for that event, and finish all the tasks you need to do before that and use the exciting event as a motivation.

The next day, I was happy to try and increase my motivation to get this assignment done with and put in all my effort to doing really well, as I was looking forward to summer. I tried to use summer as a prize I would get after completing and presenting my assignment. When I opened the blank presentation with only questions in it, that I had started the day before, I looked for key words in the questions and re-read the question over and over until I understood where to find the answers.

The excitement of summer starting made me push through and read the book again paying careful attention to the details while I kept the questions I had to answer in mind. Our teacher announced that history class was over, and we would be heading to math in 10 minutes. I didn't realize how fast the time went by when

I was working so hard. I was looking forward to school ending, so I could work on my project some more.

The Oregon Trail
THE WESTERN EXPANSION
By Taanvi

It was the weekend, and we decided to go cherry picking because we enjoyed it as a family, and knew that our grandparents would enjoy it as well. It was so hot. But we picked so many cherries, and took lots of pictures. We picked all sorts of cherries from the farm and did some taste testing along the way. It was nice to spend time outside and relax while seeing the trees and greenery in the distance. It was so calming and peaceful picking the cherries from the trees and really observing them. Because there was nothing else that was on my mind at that time and I was able to talk with my family. It was so relaxing and the perfect activity after all the stress of school.

As soon as we got home, our mom started to make cherry jam, and my sister and I made our favorite, scones. After they were done, we cut the hot scones, spread butter, and on top of the melting butter we put fresh cherry jam (yes, it's as good as it sounds)!

They next day, my mom brought me to the hospital to check my breathing and chest pain. They ran a lot of tests, and did some x-rays to check my body's reaction to my breathing. After about a half hour passed, the doctor said that everything was ok and normal, and that I should do some meditation and calming exercises.

So, I decided that if that pain ever happened again that I would do the square breathing technique that my mom taught me in Ireland during her afterschool meditation classes. When she first guided us on the technique, she said to imagine a square, and follow along the sides. While imagining one of the sides she told us to count to 4, and breathe in...1..2..3..4. Then, she said to hold for four beats, and breathe out for the next four, and finally, rest for the remaining fourth side for four beats. I realize now looking back we may pick others anxiousness no matter how much we prepare ourselves. Breathing gently brought me back to a safe space.

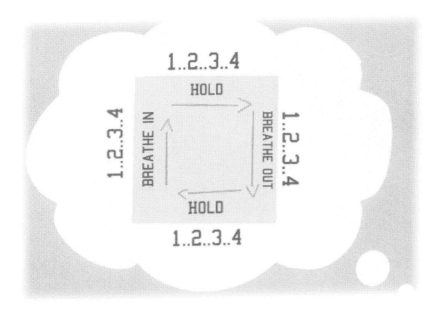

Square breathing

Square breathing, also known as box breathing is a great and quick technique to relieve stress and feel instantly calmer. It's used frequently in high stress jobs or highly stressful jobs, and is known to be a terrific breathing exercise.

This doesn't take long, and it's great to use your imagination and breath at the same time. Try it out, and see the impact. If you like it, repeat it and keep it in your tool kit.

Step 1
Take a minute out of your work, and be calm without any distractions.

Step 2
Imagine a box, and each side has 1,2,3,4 across it, the first side you breathe in for four counts, then the next side you hold for four counts, the next you exhale for four counts and then rest for four counts.

Step 3
You can repeat this as often as you would like, and enjoy the relaxation.

A couple weeks passed, and my slideshow was complete. My teacher gave us the dates to present with our table group. I was looking forward to sharing all my hard work and new learnings. The teacher announced that my Oregon trail presentation would be the next day. I shared all the information I learned when I researched about the pioneers on lives on the Oregon trail, the supplies they brought and how long it took them to go on the trail. When I was done presenting, I listened to my peers in my table group present and share their learnings. The end of the day, I learned a lot more and was delighted when I scored full points. I knew that my hard work and motivation paid off.

Now, I could allow myself to be excited that there were only two weeks until summer vacation, so I created a checklist of what I wanted to do over the summer. My sister was also happy for the summer to come and was looking forward to a nice long break, and to spend more time with me.

During the last week of school my teacher showed movies and let us play games as we completed wrapping up our subjects. Time went by so fast; the last day of school arrived quickly. I got up and ready in the morning for the last day of 4th grade. I was shocked how fast the school year had gone by, and relieved that summer started the next day. When I went to school with a big smile on my face, my teacher explained our plan for the day. First, we would watch a movie and play games with each other, then, eat our lunch, and lastly get our yearbooks signed with other classes.

When we were watching the movie, a couple of kids I sometimes talked to during recess invited me to sit with them. I was so happy that I was starting to make friends. We had one more thing to do which was yearbook signing. I didn't have a yearbook for anyone to sign, because I came in half-way through the school year. I thought I would be left out and bored, but my peers asked me if I could sign their yearbooks. This made me feel included and I was delighted that people wanted me to sign their yearbooks. I have to say, that school year was a lot of fun, and very unique. As soon as the bell rang for the end of the day, I was so happy and was already in a summertime mood.

Summer

When I was walking home with my sister from school for the last time, we both were really excited and happy for summer. When we reached home after a ten-minute walk, we threw our backpacks on the stairs and lay down on the stairs relaxed, but also pumped for the long summer break.

Every summer since we could remember, as a family we would all go to India to see our grandparents, but this year since our grandparents came over, we didn't go, and decided to go the next year. It was so nice having them over, and was really special to us.

As the next day I didn't have anything to do, and had lots more free-time, I decided that I would use it for something I would enjoy, like playing in the neighborhood park. I brought along my sister, and my next-door neighbor that I go to school with. We three biked down the slope and into the park. The weather was quite hot and the monkey bars were slippery, but I enjoyed playing around.

We three talked, and other kids we didn't recognize, who live in our neighborhood came. After introducing ourselves, we all played grounders. It was a new game to me and my sister. We played games on the swings, and ran around, biked and also played tip the can. Before we knew it all the kids' parents called them in for dinner, and one by one all the kids left. As it was getting dark outside, my sister, my friend and I cycled back up the slope and agreed how fun that was.

Laughing and playing games while sharing stories, hours went by, and that's what I loved about the summer, not being on schedule. I hoped to do this every day, and just chillax.

I enjoyed this so much, that I went almost every day, and it was really fun to come up with new games and play them while bringing more people in.

Some days we would get home after playing outside at around eight, if our parents were free we would gather and play board games. This became our routine. This is exactly how I like spending my me time, with my family and friends just chillaxing.

Me-time

Extra time is your me-time. You can spend it any way you like, with anyone. It's your time to relax and just be proud of and appreciate yourself.

Be your awesome self and appreciate yourself for getting through every day. Celebrate you!

Step 1
Make time for yourself, and add in your schedule so you will put aside time for that.

Step 2
Brainstorm what you would like to do, like paint, draw, exercise, talk, journal, or the many other possibilities.

Step 3
When you are having your me-time, be in the moment and try to be in the present so you can enjoy it to the fullest.

Somedays, it was either raining or our parents would be busy with work, and not being able to go outside and play games made us think of other things we could do. So, when we did get to go outside and play games it made me feel more appreciative and grateful for the fun I was having. In Ireland, my sister and I would rarely watch TV... only our favorite shows... But here, we had so many choices of different shows and movies whenever we wanted! We loved spending time exploring all the options.

During the summer, I kept in touch with my friends in Ireland. We exchanged letters, called, and had video chats. Because of different time zones, only 11 am would work for us to call, and during school days I couldn't. But, during summer, I had more time to talk with Angelica, and I was so thankful for that.

In our neighborhood park one day, all the families came together and had a potluck, where we all brought different snacks. My sister and I, as well as other kids played in the playgrounds, while the adults all gathered around and talked. It was lots of fun, and I really enjoyed getting to see lots of people, and be in a community. In Ireland we would always go to family gatherings with our parents' friends who had kids our age and we enjoyed playing with. But when we moved here, this potluck was the first time we found people we enjoyed talking to and playing with. It was a great community building event, and it was really nice to socialize with other kids in the neighborhood and just spend time talking with them as well.

My parents made lots of friends, and the next weekend, we were invited to join a barbecue by a family. We were really excited because we loved barbecues and spending time with friends as a family.

That summer week went by while we were doing some painting, biking and games. The family that invited us over that weekend planned a very nice and yummy barbecue.

My sister and I didn't have anything planned, so we signed up for some library events. We attended an in-person build a robot, and a space painting workshop. It was so exciting, and was something fun to look forward to. Some days, my sister and I would try baking something with our mom like cakes, muffins, and our personal favorite banana bread.

During the summer, six weeks of break felt so nice and long. The summer in America was really hot, unlike in Ireland where in one day there are so many different conditions, like some sun, rain, hail, and wind. I honestly don't prefer the heat and would choose cold over hot any day, because when you're cold you can add more clothes, but when you're hot there's nothing you can do. Although if you think about it, there are beaches, and swimming pools that keep you cool in the heat. Talking about swimming pools, my sister and I love swimming. In Ireland, we went to a swimming club every Saturday, and learned a lot about swimming techniques. We apply what we learned whenever we go to the swimming pool.

Over the summer, we sometimes went to the swimming pools and all of us enjoyed it a lot. It was so much fun that whenever we went, we would have the best time enjoying the water. We spent more time with grandparents, and talked to them, as well as gardened and did so many other things we enjoyed. I had the most fun doing some hand creations. After watching "Stuck In The Middle," I got inspired to create an invention like the ones Harley Diaz does, and loved the idea of making something out of junk materials, So, I took a box and collected some boxes and old pens and decided to create something, and before I knew it, I was able to unexpectedly invent some really cool fidget toys. I enjoyed spending the time doing that because it was creative, and also very hands on, like the cardboard bookshelf I made for my sister. Somedays I was really bored, and my sister and I weren't sure what to do together. So we would just spend hours on our phones looking for ideas for what to do, and then we decided to ask our mom for some art ideas, and then we would finally get working on a fun project.

As the end of August was approaching, we got an email from the school about the curriculum and important school dates to remember, I was really excited as I kind of missed getting a project to work on and being able to have a to do list. My sister was going to start 7th grade in September, and I was starting 5th grade. I was looking forward to the last year of Elementary school, and was excited to go to school now because I knew more about the structure. Although, there was a part of me that wasn't looking forward to going back to school because of taking the SBAC again, and getting a bigger workload than 4th grade (and I thought 4th grade was hard). Also, I didn't have friends that I had a connection and bond with, and having that would have made me look forward to meeting my friends, like in Ireland. But I didn't have that. Here the students in the class change every year, and the friends I had one year might not come into the next year's class and that upset me. Also, when I scanned through the 5th grade curriculum, I was a little overwhelmed by all the things we would be learning. I felt I was carrying a burden on my shoulders and my mind was feeling like a heavy weight. I didn't know if anyone else felt this way as well. Typically, I enjoy school, but the start of school, when we learn how the year will be and everything we will be learning, is all too much for me.

That night, when I got into bed I tossed and turned and wasn't able to fall asleep even though I was tired. My mind was occupied and busy with managing all my thoughts about school starting up in just two weeks. After what felt like hours, my eyes finally shut and when I opened them up again it was morning. But I still didn't want the feeling where I couldn't sleep, because it made me feel uncomfortable and I only focused on the negative aspect of school. I didn't tell my parents or sister yet because I thought it would go away if I convinced myself that it wasn't there and just ignored it. But the same sleep issue happened the next night.

To stop these thoughts affecting my sleep, I googled "What should I do if I am not able to sleep?" There were many YouTube videos and I clicked a yoga video. I played it, and they showed a technique called Belly Breathing, I remembered learning about this when I did yoga as an after-school activity in Ireland. When I watched the video, I followed along, sitting down in a comfortable position, and closing my eyes, I put my hands on my belly, and closed my lips. I followed along and took a deep slow breath in, through my nose and filled my belly with air making it look like a balloon, then as guided, I breathed out and slowly popped that big balloon in my belly.

When I repeated this technique when I tried to sleep, I felt my eye lids starting to get heavy, and before I knew it, I fell asleep calmly without any negative thoughts about school popping in. After experiencing how good and beneficial that belly breathing was, I kept that tip bookmarked in my mind to remember if I experienced the same feeling again. It was like a sack being lifted, and I felt so relieved knowing that I had the belly breathing trick up my sleeve.

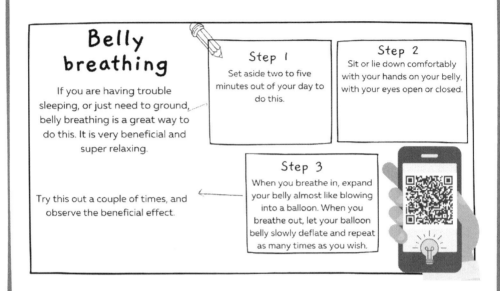

Belly breathing

If you are having trouble sleeping, or just need to ground, belly breathing is a great way to do this. It is very beneficial and super relaxing.

Try this out a couple of times, and observe the beneficial effect.

Step 1
Set aside two to five minutes out of your day to do this.

Step 2
Sit or lie down comfortably with your hands on your belly, with your eyes open or closed.

Step 3
When you breathe in, expand your belly almost like blowing into a balloon. When you breathe out, let your balloon belly slowly deflate and repeat as many times as you wish.

When I woke up the next morning, I was deciding whether or not to tell my family about my thoughts. I made a decision; I thought it was best I tell them because in our family we share our emotions with each other, and I feel comfortable sharing things because I know it's a safe place. Additionally, I thought they might have other ways to help if it came up again. So at breakfast, I told my mom, dad and sister that I was having a hard time thinking about and being nervous about school. I felt much better after telling them this and it felt good to not keep it in because it was hard to deal with it alone. When I explained this they listened and mentioned some things that helped them in these situations. Writing down the worries, blowing the worrying away, and kicking the worries off were a few they mentioned for me to try if I ever needed.

Movie

I decided that because summer was ending so soon, I would enjoy the last two weeks and have lots of fun. So, I did one of my favorite things, watching movies. I watched the movie "Wonder" with my sister. While watching the movie, I began to think how hard it was for Auggie (main character) to change his thoughts about the people he was with and be understanding. He also tried to think positively about things like school, and his friendships. I connected with this message, and was amazed when I realized that if I could change my thoughts to be positive that it would help me to not concentrate on the negative about anything, like going to 5th grade.

While watching the movie, I thought about converting my negative thoughts, like how I had no friends to hang out with, and searching for the positive thought that it would be an exciting challenge to make new friends, and that I would be able to because I am kind and funny. I set positive affirmations as well like, "This year will be fun," "I will enjoy and get excited for school," and "I will do my best in school." With that change in mindset, the butterflies in my stomach slowly faded away and the smile in my face brightened.

Negative to Positive

When you feel yourself thinking negatively, or overly about something, and it makes you feel uncomfortable. Try this technique.

It may feel weird taking time to do this, but it can help to bring a big smile on your face and make you feel better.

Step 1
Allow all of your thoughts to be heard and seen.

Step 2
When you encounter a negative thought, understand the thought and what it's saying

Step 3
Try to think about the overall picture, and find something that's positive or excites you. If you can't find anything, look for other thoughts and come back to this one later.

I enjoyed the ending of summer so much, and was getting excited for school to start. I wasn't looking forward to getting more homework. Since I knew school would be stressful, I planned to continue taking breaks and five-minute meditation sessions that would help me to be grounded like I did last year.

I was feeling anxious about school starting, about the transition to a new grade, and I was worried about making new friends. In Ireland, I would be excited for school all the time because it meant more playdates and spending time with my bestie. But, without having such close friends, I was starting to feel very anxious and worried. I was also worried that I would have a new teacher, since my one last year was really kind and made me feel comfortable and helped me to understand better.

The first day of school arrived and I walked into my classroom like all my new classmates. As I sat down, I saw a couple of my classmates and friends that I was familiar with from last year, and I was so happy to have them in my class again. The day started off by getting to know each other, and listening to my teacher go over the syllabus for each subject. I was really excited when I learned that we would be writing our own personal narrative later in the school year. I was looking forward to lunch so I could talk with my classmates and friends. The girls I sat with for the last day of school invited me to play with them during recess, I was delighted and so thankful to have such kind people in my class who were so welcoming.

As we were getting to understand how the school year would be, and how it would be for 5th graders, the bell rang. The second I stepped out of my classroom I waited for my sister to come to walk home. I sighed with relief that I had made it through my first day of my last year of elementary school. When my sister came, as we both were walking, we spent the whole time talking about our day and the exciting parts we were looking forward to.

Learning about decimals in math, the Declaration of Independence in social studies, soccer in fitness, how to write stories in English and learning to play the recorder in music - it was all so much fun at school.

At school, during our library time, our library teacher told us about the new project we will be starting. She said the project was to create an infographic about whatever we are interested in. She showed us her example and gave us time to think of what we would like to make ours about. I was brainstorming some ideas, like smartphone usage, favorite ice-cream flavors, and most-watched TV shows. She then said, if we have at least 2 ideas, that we could look at the stats, to narrow our ideas down. So, I looked online first about smartphone usage and found some cool facts about what people use their smartphones for, which ages most use them, and how many people use them. It was so interesting to dig deeper. As, I was so interested in this, I finalized my decision for the project to be about this. At the right moment, it was lunchtime. I was so excited for lunch because right after lunch we have recess, and recess is so much fun because I made new friends and we played in the playground with a bouncy ball. I was so happy to have found such nice, kind friends. After recess, we wrapped up our school day with math and history. That was a very exciting day. I told my parents and sister about the project, and I was really excited. I felt a bit nervous, because I wasn't sure how to make an infographic and whether I could get all my information done in time... Also, I didn't understand how to site my sources. But I decided to ask all my questions in class the next day.

Since it was just the start of the school year, my teacher gave less work which was really nice, because I got to spend more time with my grandparents and I could listen to their stories. It was super fun and I enjoyed chatting with them. I felt relieved that I didn't have to feel overwhelmed with work and that we were thankfully slowly easing into the school year projects.

In school, there was an assembly where middle schoolers came and showed their talent playing different instruments. The music director said that there were classes for 5th graders to come into the middle school in the mornings and learn how to play. There were many instruments shown; flute, violin, tuba, saxophone, trombone, French horn, trumpet, etc. It was so cool to see all the instruments and the songs played with them. Then we were handed information about dates and where to rent instruments if we were interested in being part of the program. I showed this to my family when I got home because I liked the instruments and wanted to learn how to play one. My mom asked me which instrument I liked. I said I loved the flutist that played the Star Wars song, and the violinist that played Havana.

Later that week we went to the music shop and asked which would be better for beginners. The person in the shop suggested we rent a violin and a flute, bring them home and decide once I played a little on each. So, we took both. I looked at how to play the instruments on YouTube and listened to some music. I liked the music the flute produced. In the past at school, I had learned to play the recorder and tin whistle and they are a little like the flute. So, the next day we headed back to the shop and returned the violin. I was so looking forward to the next week when the morning classes started, and the best part was that it was at the middle school my sister goes to which is right beside my elementary school. I tried to ignore all my thoughts, like I wasn't sure who else was going, and if I would be super late, or how things would go in the class, if the band teacher would be nice, and if I would be going into the right class. I had a million worries of the unknown, and tried to ignore them, and not worry too much about it.

On my first day of band class, my sister guided me to the band room, then said good luck and headed back to her friends. I walked into the classroom and saw some of the kids from my school, sitting in a circle. Our band teacher introduced himself, then we all introduced ourselves. Next our band teacher talked about what we would be doing. He also said that woodwinds (such as flute, clarinet, piccolo, oboe, saxophone, etc.) and percussion (drum, xylophone, tambourine, marimba, gong, etc.) would be in different groups. He said the woodwinds would be taught the basics of their instruments by the assistant teacher in the room right next door, and our band director would teach the percussionists. I was so excited to learn how to assemble our instruments, but at the same time wasn't sure if I needed any background in music to be able to read sheet music for songs or not. So, I asked the other flute players if they knew, and just like me, they said they didn't. This made me feel more comfortable and slowly my worries were fading away, and I felt more relaxed and was enjoying the class.

The morning class was over already, it felt very quick. I was looking forward to the next class when we were going to learn how to play our instruments. Music is always fun and engages my brain and hand movements. I enjoy learning different tunes and the sounds an instrument can produce. My teacher keeps us all engaged and makes class very interactive and that motivates me. My favorite part is working as a class on every song, and hearing what all the different instruments sound like in one room.

Author Visit

Later that week, my sister shared some very exciting news, she said that the author Emma Shevah would be coming to her middle school and that elementary school kids could walk there and listen. I was so excited because even though I don't often read books, I love hearing the authors' perspectives on how they write. It greatly inspires me because I love writing, and it's my goal one day to publish a book. I signed up and was so excited.

In 2017 when my mom published her book I felt proud and in that moment I felt like writing a book too. I went to my room and wrote a short story of 10 pages and binded it into a book format with main cover page and gave to my family. That was my first unofficial book for off the records information.

The next week, the big day finally arrived. When I walked into the library, I saw so many books, and shelves, I thought it was pretty cool. But my sister always talks to me about how many books there are, and also how kind the librarians were. When I scanned the room to see where the librarians were, they walked out of their office and greeted us all, and directed us to the seating area. They were definitely as kind as my sister described.

In the seating area, there were chairs lined up, and we all took a seat. Then the author, Emma Shevah, pulled up a slideshow on the TV. She introduced herself, by saying that she was born and raised in London. She said that her father was from Thailand and her mom from Ireland. That moment when she said she was part Irish, I felt so happy. For some reason, it made me feel more comfortable and excited to see someone who was connected to Ireland. It made me think about how someone can do such an awesome thing like write multiple books, no matter where you're from. She said she loved writing and she had published many books including "Dream On, Amber," "Dara Palmer's Major Drama" and "What Lexie Did."

Then, she talked about what inspired her in writing these books. She explained about some of her friends, her life experiences, and everyday things that inspired her. I was so interested in the process of how she sat down, brainstormed, and took the time to write these creative stories. I thought to myself, she has published so many books already; she must be really patient to revise, edit and recreate things. Because I want to be an author, I kept notes in my head for future use. I tried to remember the most important one, which is to be patient (the hardest one for me). Next, she showed us all the books she had written and passed them around for us to see. Then, one of the librarians came up and said these books are available for check-out in the middle school and our elementary school library. I really wanted to check the book out and try my best to get through the whole book.

When Emma wrapped up her speaking and showing, she opened up to questions from us. I raised my hand and asked "If we want to be an author, what can we do now?" She said it was a great question and added that I should just keep writing and getting creative by practicing writing many different stories. After that, the thought of writing a story got into my mind, and I decided I would write a fantasy. I felt like asking a million more questions - most importantly I wanted to ask her if she ever felt de-motivated or experienced what some people call "author's block." But, I decided to keep the question on hold as she was wrapping up her talk.

Then, we said goodbye, and walked back to school and to continue with our class. But, in my mind, the excitement of wanting to write a story lingered, and I also looked forward to telling my family that she was part Irish!

The Holidays

It was already December, and the holidays were so close. I was so looking forward to a nice long break for two weeks, going out to a hotel with my grandparents.

At school, we had an English assignment. It was about choosing a species of animal as our choice reading assignment. I was happy because I love choice projects, but I knew it would be harder for me to choose an animal, as I don't have any favorite animal.

We all went to the school monitors and logged onto a site where we could see all the animals we could choose from, when we clicked on the animal icons, we could hear the noises they make and see the live video cams to see their behavior. To brainstorm some ideas for myself, I thought of snakes, dolphins, and whales as they seemed like the most interesting, and looking into them, I did some background research for all three, and in the end narrowed it to dolphins, because I wanted to learn how they could communicate underwater and thought they were cool creatures. I realized choosing an animal wasn't as hard as I thought it would be, and that was nice. So, when I looked more into dolphins, I found some interesting facts. Our library teacher gave us a quick walk-through of our projects. She said that once we checked out books, and got more online information about our topics, we could create a paper of what we had learned. I was looking forward to this because I was excited read more about dolphins.

After recess that day, in PE my teachers announced that we would be having a really interesting unit ahead of us. We would be learning different jump rope styles, and with a partner or independently we had to create a jump rope routine and show it to them for points. I asked one of my friends if they would like to partner. Jump rope was something we didn't really learn or do in Ireland for PE.

We would typically play running games or dodgeball. But I was looking forward to creating a jump rope routine and spending time with my friends while doing so. Class was over, and next was recess. During recess, my friends and I all got jump ropes from the recess box and started practicing our routines. It was so much fun.

When I got home, my sister was at piano lessons, which gave me time to make a birthday scrapbook for her, because her birthday was over break. I was excited to work on her cards and scrapbook. It was a great way to relax and do something nice for her 13th birthday.

The weeks were over so fast, and we wrapped up our slideshow for animals in the library, and my friend and I got full points on our jump rope routine. (We did think it was pretty awesome.) Next up was a well-deserved break.

Break was so much fun. We celebrated my sister's birthday and had fun with friends at home. The space-themed cake made the day even yummier! She loved my gifts and enjoyed flipping through the scrapbook I created for her. A couple of days after, we all started packing our bags for our trip to Lake Chelan. It was our grandparent's first time in the US, and our first time going on a little vacation with them here. We were all so excited, but we weren't looking forward to the four hour drive.

The next morning, we woke up early and started straight away on our long drive. We packed snacks, coloring pencils, paper, and some fidget toys. The drive was more fun than expected. We blasted the speakers in our car, slept, and talked. Four hours were over, and we were finally in our hotel room laying on the beds. After logging into the Wi-Fi, we searched for restaurants nearby and picked one out. The food was really good, and it was fun to chillax. The week went by doing the same things, but one day it snowed! It was so fun because we could play in the snow together with my grandparents. We made snowmen and threw snowballs, then we celebrated Christmas at the hotel, ate outside, and opened our gifts. It was so fun, and I loved relaxing and not needing to think of school. But soon there was New Year's, and our trip ended. We drove home and unpacked. It was kind of sad because we had had so much fun, but we still had three days before school started again. During the weekend, we played with our Christmas toys, watched movies, and celebrated the beginning of 2020.

It was Sunday night. Typically, these nights are hard for me because I enjoy the weekends so much and then to think the next day is school again is difficult sometimes, especially after a long, fun-packed break.

Sometimes when I have nothing to look forward to, it makes it harder for me to be excited about school. But luckily this time I was excited to see my friends and get back to work on my projects.

Usually, when I feel upset or anxious about going to school on Monday, I talk it out with my parents and they help me to think of the exciting things in the week - like a meeting or a school event. I have learned not to hold it for too long no matter how big or small it could feel in that moment. But this time, without talking to them, a positive perspective came to me on my own and it made me happy to know that I had an inner tool to stop my anxiety and I was able to transition quickly.

That week at school, our principal told us we would be having a science fair and baking fundraiser. She said the science fair was mandatory for all 5th graders, and that we could have partners this time. I was so happy when I heard this announcement because I loved last year's science fair. The principal later announced that we can have a partner. This started to make me feel nervous about who I should choose, and how the project would come out depending on which friend I chose, and how our teamwork might be as I wasn't sure how any of my friends' studying patterns were. But I convinced myself to remember all of my experiences and how I overcame the nervousness and expanded my comfort zone. I decided to choose one of my friends that seemed like she wanted to pair up as well. Though I was nervous about what we would choose as a project and if we would both contribute equally, I was starting to get more excited about it.

Later that day, our teacher gave us some time to brainstorm ideas and select partners if we were choosing to. My partner and I opened up the computers and searched for ideas. Some of the options we found included, "Which liquids freeze faster," "Does music affect plant growth," "Which soil helps plants grow faster..." We kept searching, but decided "which liquid freezes faster" sounded the most fun. We decided with the teacher and started planning the process. First, the project sheet told us to come up with a null hypothesis, then variables, and steps on how we would conduct the experiment and record data. We sat down and opened a document and decided we would check the liquids every 15 minutes, and that we would experiment with water, coke, lemonade, milk, and vinegar.

The following week it was time to start our experiment. We came in early that day and got the ice tray and drinks ready, then we poured each one in separately to each section. Then, we put it in the freezer and set a timer for 15 minutes, so we could go check on it. Just as we finished and were ready to sit down, the rest of our classmates started coming in, and the class was starting. Then, the 15 minute timer rang. It honestly felt longer than I thought it would. We both stood on a stool to reach the mini freezer above the high cabinet where we put the ice tray. We pulled the tray out carefully and while I examined the ice/liquid formations, my partner wrote down what I told her about each liquid. Our teacher told us that we could complete 1/2 of the math worksheet, but get full points. So, in between science project timer checks, we worked through the worksheet problems we were assigned. It was really exciting when the timer rang, and we got to check. Near the end of the school day, the timer rang, and we checked like the other couple of times, but instead of resetting the timer, we turned it off and cleaned out the ice tray and threw out the empty cans. After my partner and I cleaned our desk, we quickly reflected on the experiment. We discussed that it was difficult to record the data in a consistent way, and since we kept sticking our whole finger in to check the texture of the ice after the 15 mins, we thought the data was not completely right, we learned that there are lots of variables that can affect it, so we can remember for next time. Just as we finished up our conversation, the end of school bell rang.

At home, I typed up all the data we had collected from that day into a spreadsheet, so it could be displayed on our final tri-fold. The next day, my teacher gave the whole class some time to work on our science project. My friend and I tried to be as productive as possible while having fun. First, we both got a computer from the computer charging station, and opened up a slideshow, we started typing up some of the information needed to display, wrote down our observations, and then printed it in a way we could later stick on the tri-fold board. We also printed out a data chart, showing the information in a graph format.

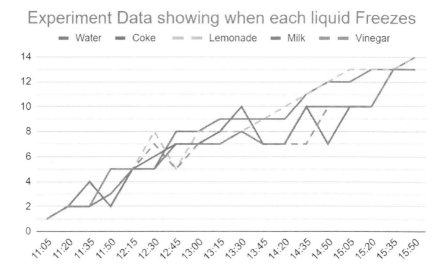

	11:05	11:20	11:35	11:50	12:15	12:30	12:45	1:00	1:15	1:30	1:45	2:20	2:35	2:50
Water	liquid	cold liquid	cold liquid	slushy	slush	slush	bottom slush	bottom slush	bottom ice	bottom ice	bottom ice	bottom ice	1/2 rock ice	3/4 hard ice
Coke	liquid	cold liquid	thicker liquid	cold liquid	slush	very slushy	hard slush	hard slush	bottom slush	rock slush	hard slush	hard slush	rock slush	hard slush
Lemonade	liquid	cold liquid	cold liquid	slushy	slush	bottom slush	slush	bottom slush	bottom slush	bottom slush	bottom ice	rock slush	1/2 rock ice	3/4 hard ice
Milk	liquid	cold liquid	cold liquid	soft liquid	slush	slushy	hard slush	hard slush	hard slush	bottom slush	hard slush	hard slush	rock slush	rock slush
Vinegar	liquid	cold liquid	cold liquid	slushy	slush	hard slush	slush	hard slush	hard slush	bottom slush	hard slush	hard slush	hard slush	rock slush

Just as we had all the printouts in our hands, my teacher said we would be wrapping up and continuing this tomorrow. My friend and I were proud of how well we did this project using teamwork skills. We both jotted down what we had to complete for the project to be ready for display.

On our to do list, we wrote that we needed to print out a typed order of the steps we followed for the experiment, and we also had to complete a list of limitations we had during the project. We were looking forward to completing the project and sticking all the papers, and graphs to the board, which would be our next step after completing the task on our to do list.

Our teacher said that tomorrow was our last day to complete the science project in class, and the rest would be homework. When the next day came, my friend and I were looking forward to science time so we could complete our to do list and decorate the tri-fold board with all our data. Also, since it was our last class work time, my teacher gave more time to complete the project. We took our time and made sure we got everything required, and then submitted our project for display. Then we took some time to help our other classmates with sticking things at the last minute. We then got to relax, and chat for the remaining time. At the end of class, my teacher handed out a slip to everyone in the class with information about when the science fair and bake sale would be. Once I got home, I shared this with my parents, grandparents, and sister. They were so excited to see my science fair project, and to buy some goods from the bake sale. I couldn't wait for the science fair date to arrive, especially since everyone in school was hyping it up.

Finally, after four days, it was time for the science fair and bake sale. We all walked into the gym where the science fair projects were displayed. After a bit of searching, I found mine, and my family read through it and liked it. My partner and I were very impressed with our work. I felt like we made equal contributions and in the end it turned out great. I think it was a great experienced to partner up as there are many benefits to two minds rather than one. After we looked around at the other projects, there were some science stands. We all went to a stand where a woman had a brain in a bottle, and took the brain out and let us feel the actual brain, it was the COOLEST thing. Then, there was a student's dad who had a stall set up with a bucket of blubber and ice-cold water. He instructed my sister and me to put a glove on us, then stick our hand in the bucket of blubber, and then stick our hand in ice-cold water. When I tried this, I felt no cold whatsoever when sticking my hand into the ice-cold water; it was so interesting. He told us that it is the fat of sea mammals like whales and seals. After listening more about the science, we went over to the bake sale and got a brownie and cookie. There was also a book sale going on in the school, I wanted to see what types of books there were, and then I saw an animals national geographic jokes book, and wanted to buy it. I also found something I thought my sister would like. It was about the galaxy and stars. We bought both these books and were so excited to use them. At around 9 pm everyone started heading out. After taking pictures near the project with my friend, we all left.

That week was pretty tough, so I was really happy on the weekend to be able to spend time with my friends in the neighborhood park and watch a movie. But my parents suggested we all go a to a local blueberry picking farm.

My sister and I weren't too excited to go because we just wanted to stay home and binge watch, and play with friends, and didn't want to go on a long drive and bear the heat. But we decided to give it a try. When we got there after a long drive, there were so many blueberries, and so many varieties, like highbush, lowbush, hybrid half-high, and rabbit eye. We all picked up a bucket and set on our way to pick as many blueberries as we could. After about an hour, it was starting to get hot, and we all became tired. We decided to pay for the blueberries, head home, and eat some ice cream.

The weekend was really entertaining, and was packed with so much excitement. Though it wasn't super fun, we still gave it a try and it was a different experience. Having a weekend with things planned actually helped to take my mind off things. That was the best part - to just be in the present moment. It made me realize that the things we do on a daily basis can help become distractors from all the negative thinking. Even though I wanted to play and not go blueberry picking, going had a positive impact and brought in a lot more excitement to me which I may not have experienced doing the usual, like playing with friends in the park.

School Release

The weekend was over, and Monday arrived. Monday morning, after my dad took my sister to school, and drove to work, my mom and I started walking to my school. It's always so fun to walk with her, and I really enjoy talking to her on our 15-minute morning walks to school. After she dropped me, I went to the playground for morning recess. My friends started coming in as well. We were all playing on the swings. When I checked my Fitbit to see how many more minutes till school started, there were 10 minutes. Just then, some parents came in and started collecting their kids. I was super confused because we weren't told anything, and when I went to go ask the recess supervisor, he told all of us that school was being canceled for the day. I was starting to feel very anxious because I wasn't sure how to get home. I decided to text my mom to ask what I should do. She replied that her friend from our neighborhood would collect me and her younger daughter. After waiting for about 5 minutes, my mom's friend came and picked me and her daughter up. I felt so much lighter and calmer as the butterflies in my stomach released.

Then, she dropped me home and I just watched TV. And glad my grandparents with us I could spend extra time with them. After some time when my mom's work ended, I asked her why the school was released early. She explained that someone in the science fair had tested positive for COVID and that they wanted to release everyone in case it passed on. I connected this to what my dad was talking about earlier after what he read on the news about covid when he explained this to my sister and me. I was a little bit worried because I didn't want to get COVID because some people were suffering a lot because of it. Then, my mom told my sister and me that we shouldn't worry, that we were strong and healthy. So, I tried not to worry about it and just be as safe as I could.

While eating dinner that night, my parents got another email saying the person with a positive case was being quarantined, and that we could go back to school. The email also said that anyone feeling sick or ill should stay home for everyone's safety. They also added that in the school there would be safety measures put into place.

The next day my teacher welcomed us and gave us a squirt of hand sanitizer. Then, she talked to us about the emails our parents were getting and asked all of us to signal to her with hand movements how much we knew about COVID, she said to do a thumbs up if we knew what it was, a middle hand if we kind of knew, and a thumbs down if we didn't know. I kept my hand in the middle position because I didn't know some of the details. Since most of us had our hands down or in the middle, she decided it would be best if she showed us a Dr. Binocs video about COVID that the school

district sends out to all teachers. The video gave information about how it was presumed to have started and what it is, as well as other information about it.

Then, she showed us a poster of some of the protocols the CDC was recommending to stay safe. She talked it through with us, and also had discussion time to share our feelings. I hadn't reflected on it or thought about how it made me feel, but I did then. After thinking, I realized that it made me feel stressed since all the news was buzzing about it. I felt anxious, because I was not sure how it would affect my life or how long it would last. I was also feeling some fear because I didn't want to get COVID and hated the thought of having it.

Then, my teacher started talking about if school were to be closed how it would work, and how the district's worst case scenario option was to do online learning.

When that very different school day was over, my sister said that they were talking about an online learning option if the COVID cases got higher. I didn't fully understand what online learning meant, but I hoped that we wouldn't have to do it because I liked how things were. I started to feel tense, stressed and anxious about what would happen because there was so much uncertainty. This whole thing was new to me and everyone else, so no one could give me clarity.

When we reached home, had our snack and finished homework, we headed outside, biked and played in the playground together for a while. We decided to head back home since it was getting dark. After heading home, I felt more relaxed and distracted from everything that was going on. It felt good to do sports because it helped to distract me from my thoughts, and it was great exercise.

Honestly, even though I don't like biking that much, I really enjoy spending time with my sister chatting about things like cooking, baking, and school projects. Biking makes me feel serene, and it releases emotions, like any other sports as well.

In the morning, my parents got another email from the school district. They told my sister and me that the email said that COVID cases had been rapidly growing. Taking this into consideration, the district made a decision to temporarily go to online learning for three weeks. The email said that all students would get two weeks off from school while the staff and teachers figured out how to make online school work. After hearing this, the first thing that came to my mind was the excitement of not having school for two whole weeks.

At the same time, I was feeling sad about having to do temporary online learning after, and also that more people were suffering from COVID. But I just wanted to push those thoughts behind, and try enjoying these two weeks.

For these two weeks, I was thinking of so many ideas of projects my sister and I could do. The annoying thing was we were all in lockdown and couldn't go outside. This was such an unusual experience, because we would usually go out for movies, or farms, or restaurants.

Because of COVID, now we couldn't do any of our normal activities and felt stuck inside. We just had to cope for the next two weeks being inside, and trying to think of indoor activities to do daily.

Some of the ideas I brainstormed included making fidget toys out of household items, watching movies, and playing games with my grandparents. My mom suggested that we could do art when her work meetings at home were over. The first week my sister and I watched a couple of Disney movies, and Indian movies with my grandparents.

When our mom and dad finished their work Zoom meetings, we did some acrylic painting with my mom. After finally thinking of something to paint, we got right to it and let our creative thoughts flow. We also chatted with each other, enjoying each other's company.

Art

Feel like doing something, but not sure what? Well, if you're bored Art is a great way to spend time having fun. There are many different types of art, and you can keep experimenting until you find your area of interest. There are various different ways to spend time doing art, here are a few.

There are so many more ideas than listed, but there are just some of them! Doing art is really relaxing, and doing it with my family members makes it more fun and it's nice to have company sometimes.

Way 1
Free art, do anything that comes to your mind

Way 2
Try out some really cool art painting you like

Way 3
Try a new kind of art, and learn about the art

With my dad, and sister, I learned some Java coding, it was fun to try to understand the commands. I was confused about a lot of things, but slowly with some patience (which was definitely not easy), I was able to create some cool coding projects after looking at some YouTube videos explaining commands. The second week went by like the first, filled with lots of projects.

Handmade Creations

Have some free time during break or while watching TV? Well, you can give hand creations a try, there are so many different things you can do to keep your hands busy, so give some of these ideas a try.

Try these hand making ideas, and brainstorm more! Doing hand made activities really helps to relax and be grounded, and it's a great way to be creative and just focus on one thing at a time.

Step 1
Make some random Fidget toys with scrap pieces.

Step 2
Think of and Create inventions.

Step 3
Play with Rubik's cubes.

On Sunday after the two weeks, we received an email with a plan regarding online learning. The email said that we would be using a platform called Google Classroom, and once we logged into our classroom, we would find classroom assignments, Zoom meeting links and resources like office hours booking.

After reading that email, I was so nervous to log in to google classroom, as I didn't understand any of the technology and was super confused. But, when I logged into my classroom, I saw many of my friends and classmates logged in already and it made me feel so much more calm. I also saw the meeting Zoom link posted for tomorrow morning, as well as the schedule. I started to look around clicking different buttons, exploring the platform, and found it really cool. I was looking forward to seeing how things would go tomorrow, and hoped it would go well, as it was my first time using the new software.

Online Learning

It was Monday, the FIRST DAY OF ONLINE LEARNING! I was so excited because I got to sleep in longer. It was definitely a weird experience, because we would be going to school from home. There was just one thing I was nervous about, and that was being late, so I decided that I would go to every meeting 10 minutes early, so I would be on time, and not have to be late.

After eating breakfast, and heading upstairs to my room I logged into the zoom link(10 minutes early). I saw so many more classmates in the meeting, and my teacher. After about 10 minutes of waiting, when more of my classmates joined, my teacher shared some zoom expectations, and how class would function online for the next 3 weeks. Just before morning class time ended, one of my classmates raised their hand and asked how long this online learning would be, and our teacher responded unsurely saying hopefully not long, but at this point she said nobody knows. This made me start to feel upset because that meant I didn't know when I could see my friends in person again, and I loved talking to them at school. I really felt like there were so many things I was going to miss like recess time, and having lunch with my friends, as well as getting a jump start to each day. But I was trying to look for exciting things about online learning like more sleeping time, lunch with family, learning technology, getting to turn off my camera sometimes in class, being able to get snacks whenever, and also getting to spend more free time after school.

After that morning class time was over, it was time for lunch and I got to eat lunch with all my family, because my parents also had their office from home. After eating lunch, it was time to return to my desk and log in again for my school afternoon session. This was when we were introduced to some of our future assignments. After that, the school day was over, and we didn't get any assignments yet, because the teacher wanted all of us to get used to online learning first. But she said the following week we would get some homework and assignments.

After that day, I felt so strained by watching my computer and staying in my room for the whole time. I didn't like having to sit like that because moving around makes me feel less sleepy and tired.

Finally, after the long week of online learning was over, I realized that I didn't like it as much as I thought, because I couldn't talk to any of my classmates, and it was less interactive. I also felt very bored after class because there was so much time, but I didn't feel like doing anything. So, I watched TV because it's the easiest thing to do, but it made me feel gloomy and more tired because I watched it for way too long and my eyes started hurting.

I also felt anxious because I kept thinking I would be late to class or miss a Zoom. I was also very uncertain how many days this would go on for, and hoped it would end soon because I didn't like this change.

The next week of school was comparatively better, because we had homework, and were introduced to a choice project where we could choose what to write an essay about. But I still had more time, so during lunch that Friday, I discussed with my family some ideas of what I could do, and they said we could do art after my mom's office time ends, and I could do some sports or do a long-term project. I loved all these ideas, especially the last option of a long-term project, I liked the sound of that, and brainstormed some ideas with my sister. We came up with a list including "Obstacle Course," "Art Project," "Room Makeover," and "Musical Instrument." Out of all these, I liked the idea of a room makeover because my room looked so dull, and I had wanted to make it more colorful, since I was in my room most of the day now. After school finished up that day and I submitted my homework, I drew out some room plans, and asked my sister to help since she is really good at decorations. I was so happy to do my room makeover, and was looking forward to do it again next week after school as well.

Room Re-organize

Are you feeling bored, or stressed out? Well, maybe it's time to re-organize your room. Because, being in the same room everyday for work or for online learning can really make you feel more cluttered, and your room also gets messier which can make it harder to focus.

Taking some time to clean your room and then organize it with an organizing method and putting up some homemade decor can make it so much more organized and easier to work in. It's also a great project for over the summer, or during holidays when you're feeling bored.

Step 1
Schedule in one week of room makeover time.

Step 2
Start by deep cleaning everything like closets, and desk drawers.

Step 3
Then, look at some images online to get ideas, and put up some decor as well as organization methods around your room.

I also loved the idea of doing art because of how much it had helped me last week to relax and chat. I was looking forward to doing this after school with my mom and sister. I was eager to see how it would make me feel to do art after school, and to see how relaxed it made me.

But, before the next week arrived, it was the weekend. And this weekend, it was my dad's birthday! We all celebrated by cutting a carrot cake my sister and I baked as well as giving him all the gifts and cards we made him. He was so happy, and it was great to celebrate it with my grandparents as well. Even though we couldn't go outside and have a gathering with friends, we still tried to make it special at home.

The next day, my parents told my sister and I that we would have to drop our grandparents at the airport so they could return to India because if COVID got worse, it was less safe for them to be here and fly back after, in case the flights get canceled. After hearing this, we both were really sad because we had so much fun with them, but we understood where our parents were coming from. After they packed their suitcases, we drove to the airport, and it was hard to send them off, because they were with us for five months and we enjoyed those months with them a lot. We took a picture with them, and then they headed off. When we got home, we all were upset, and missed them, but hoped they would be safe and have a good flight.

We were so grateful that they could come over, and tried to think about everything we enjoyed with them rather than being sad that they couldn't stay longer. After that weekend, it was time for online learning week two, but this time it would be much more fun since I could look forward to doing my room makeover with my sister, and art with my sister and my mom.

Right after school was over and my sister finished her school work, we started to move around my desk and bed into a new position and did some more planning. Just as we finished up what we were doing, my parents finished their work. So, my mom, my sister and I all did some art together. We did an art challenge where we had to try include three different objects into one painting. It was so challenging to include a snowman, house, and chocolate, but we all managed to do it and they looked so different from each other. I felt so good and even though only a half hour had passed, it felt like hours had flown by. After doing art, we had some time before dinner, and since all four of us were free, we decided to play a board game. We had to choose between our three new board games, Ticket to Ride, Catan and Sorry. We all voted for Catan, and started to play this new game while reading the manual. While playing the game, we all had so much fun and enjoyed the quality family time.

During the week, we got another email from the district saying that because of the rise in COVID cases over the weeks, they made a decision to extend online learning for the next three weeks. This made me feel very sad, because I was so waiting to go back in person. But since I couldn't change anything about it, I decided to plan what I would do to make this next week the most fun. I planned some activities including room decor, biking, and also art with my mom and sister, and board games. I loved seeing so many activities I could do, and how much time I had after school.

During the week we got our first virtual project, it was another choice assignment where we could choose a topic to create a poster about. There were many different topics to choose from. After scanning them I decided to choose "Why Plastic Should Be Banned." The teacher was explaining all the different parts to the project, and which documents we should have open to check the rubrics. When we started research during the week, I started getting really stressed with the number of things we had to do. Making it even harder, because it was a different experience to do the project through because I couldn't go up to the teacher immediately for clarification. Additionally, we had lots of tasks to do like homework and assignments to submit. This made me to start feeling anxious even after school, just trying to remember if I forget to do anything I was required to complete. It started to drive me crazy as more and more things were piling up.

On Thursday, I decided to talk to my sister because maybe she was going through the same thing and could help me. She said that she was keeping sticky notes with all the things she needed to do for school. This got me thinking of creating a to do list to put all of my tasks, and then cross them off when I was done. I hoped this would help me with organizing and planning.

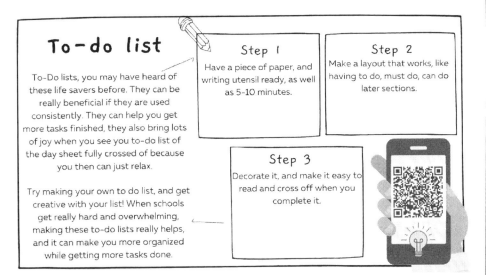

To-do list

To-Do lists, you may have heard of these life savers before. They can be really beneficial if they are used consistently. They can help you get more tasks finished, they also bring lots of joy when you see you to-do list of the day sheet fully crossed of because you then can just relax.

Try making your own to do list, and get creative with your list! When schools get really hard and overwhelming, making these to-do lists really helps, and it can make you more organized while getting more tasks done.

Step 1
Have a piece of paper, and writing utensil ready, as well as 5-10 minutes.

Step 2
Make a layout that works, like having to do, must do, can do later sections.

Step 3
Decorate it, and make it easy to read and cross off when you complete it.

I wanted to try out this new method to see if it actually would help me. So, I took a piece of paper, before school started the next day, I started to write the to do's my teacher was saying like homework math due dates, and our choice project tasks to finish before Monday. I also wrote down some questions I had that I wanted to ask my teacher while I was doing my choice project research.

That afternoon, I had all my tasks crossed of my list, and was done with school for that day so I left my computer with a sigh relief. The feeling I had was just the best. I didn't need to do anything else because I completed everything I had to do and was 100% sure. Since I had more time after completing my tasks, I wanted to do some more room makeover work, play more board games with my family, create some fidget toys and do art with my sister and mom. I was so pleased with how I did that day, and loved the idea of making a to do list. Because it helped me to switch off after school, and be more grounded and also, I had more time. I decided I would continue this for the next week.

Since I was slowly getting used to online learning, I was finding some pros and cons about it. Pros included more evening and lunch family time, getting to sleep in a bit later, less homework than normal, and also more time for hobbies. But the cons included every day being at home. It was kind of boring and tiring. Especially because online school meant we had to be glued to the screens practically all day, as well as having less social time to chat with friends during recess and throughout the school day.

I really missed seeing my friends and talking about fun things, and wanted to try to make it possible somehow, maybe online. So, I thought of having a Zoom call with my friends after school, and I texted them all and they loved the idea as well. After one of my friends made a Zoom link and shared, we all joined in after school and chatted for about an hour about things like how school was going and what each of us was doing in our classes, because we didn't all have the same teachers. We also talked about our 5th grade graduation, and we all hoped we could do it in-person because it was only two months away. After that meeting, I felt good and happy to have connected with some of my friends that I hadn't talked to for a couple of weeks. But still, it wasn't like before, and I still wished for everything to be back to normal, but I just tried to make a new normal.

Game Night

When Sunday came up, we weren't sure what we could do, but didn't want to watch TV. But I had an idea for what we could do and shared it with my sister first to see if she wanted to help me. My idea was to have a board game "night," where we play some board games, keep track of who won what, then give a prize to the ULTIMATE winner!

Family time

Taking time for enjoying yourself, and times with your family is very important! Connecting with your family. With all the things that may be going on in your life you just need time to spend with your family, and you can make it super happy and fun.

Taking time in your day to connect and talk and play games or movies freshens up your day, you can pick a time and day and make it a habit that you spend quality time and create unforgettable memories with your loving and caring family. It helps you know the value and importance of family as well as enjoying yourself!

Idea 1

Board Game Night, bring on all your family favorite board games and see who the ultimate winner of the night is.

Idea 2

Movie Night, play your best movies with the best snacks and enjoy the snuggly cozy feeling.

Idea 3

Game Night, play minute to win it challenges, and get up be active with challenges in many different games, and see who has the most wins at the end.

As soon as I told her she was really excited, and said she would love to help by making some snacks. After lunch, my sister and I told my parents that we had a surprise, and they had to come down in an hour to see it. They were pretty hyped, and decided to take a quick nap. After one hour of setting up all the games, creating the winner board, we were ready to call them down. As soon as they saw this, they were so excited to start, and after explaining some rules, we started our first family board game night. We had a blast together, and it was fun to give the ultimate winner their prize - and the snacks were good as well! After we finished, we decided we should do more of these, and maybe some other events like this together because we all enjoyed the family time we spend doing these. During

Game Night, I didn't think about anything school related and just had fun family time which really helped me to be calmer and helped me to remain in the present, after a long week.

Plastic Project

The week started, and I was really excited to get going on my project, because I wanted to learn some facts to share with my class in poster format. Even after school I worked really hard to finish up my project, as well as my other to do list items. I kept working and didn't realize how long I worked. Before going downstairs to relax, I quickly checked my phone for any school emails, and then went on to Instagram to see some reels for any inspiring ideas. I looked at things that interested me, like, satisfying videos, wood working, fruit cutting ideas and art projects. I love watching these short reels because it inspires me seeing so many others interested in what I am. After watching for ten minutes or so, I was ready to disconnect from gadgets and went downstairs to spend family time and chillax.

The next day in school we got to present our choice projects to our classmates. Some of my classmates presented before me. Theirs were really nice and all of them chose different projects. At last, the moment I had been waiting for. I got to present my choice project slide with my class. I wasn't sure if they'd like it or not, or if it was boring and too repetitive for them to even pay attention. I also wasn't confident if I did all the requirements from the rubric, but I tried my hardest and thought that was the most important thing for me. Thankfully, after the presentation, they all said that they loved it which was quite a relief. I also showed the "Start Conservation, Stop Water Pollution" video that I helped create when I was in Ireland with my dad, his friends, and my sister. It was the perfect time to share it because it connected with my topic. I was so happy people liked my project, because I worked really hard.

The next day before school, we got an email saying that since COVID cases were still steadily increasing they made a decision to complete this school year remotely, for all of our safety. And, because there was only one month of school left, they felt it was the best choice.

After reading this email, I was really upset because I hoped to see my friends again, and I probably wouldn't see most of them since next year was middle school. I realized that I wasn't going to be able to have my 5th grade graduation or the camp for 5th grade graduates. I remembered how as a 4th grader we did it for the 5th graders. The whole school created an arch and all of the 5th graders ran through it, while getting cheered on by all the lower grades. When I was in 4th grade, I was eagerly waiting to be the one underneath getting cheered for. When I realized that it would not be like that it made me upset. I also felt upset that we could not go to an overnight Camp Cedar Springs event because of COVID. I remembered how it was the biggest thing everyone talked about the whole year. I tried not to think about it, and just forget about it because I didn't want it to upset me during school. When I logged into my morning Zoom, the first topic was about how all of us were going to miss graduation, and this made all of us feel upset. It gave me some comfort, though, because I wasn't the only one going through the sadness of not having a proper 5th grade graduation. Then my teacher said we would have an online graduation party, and for Camp Cedar Springs she said they were thinking of a way to still make it happen online. This sounded pretty cool, but still we all knew that it wouldn't be the same. the same. After this discussion, my teacher started getting into our math homework check. I kept thinking of the COVID situation, and it made me really upset because I also wouldn't be able to have the primary school graduation I wanted in Ireland because I left in 4th grade, and primary school ends in 6th grade. So, I wouldn't get any graduation until middle school. My sister tried cheering me up by saying at least I get an online party, and she tried to show me the positive things like summer is coming up. This made me feel a bit better, but still it was hard to forget about what I would be missing.

After two weeks of school, we got another email just for 5th graders. The email attached a form to fill out our t-shirt size to get a graduation t-shirt, and also a Zoom link for our graduation party. The email also said that since this was the last week of school, our teacher would share the Camp Cedar Springs online event.

After the weekend, it was the last Monday of the 2019-20 school year. In our morning class we did normal math homework, then had a lunch break, and finally it was afternoon class time. Our teacher told us that for the online camp, we could watch videos of the camp leaders showing us what we would have done during camp. Watching these videos and filling out a sheet of paper on what we learned showed me what I was missing out on. But it was nice of them to even make it for us so we didn't completely miss out.

After school that day, I had no homework because we had no more assignments due for the rest of the week, and my teacher said we would just watch movies, and I was really excited because there was finally something to look forward to. It was the second to last day of school, and in the mail, I got a package addressed to me from school. After eagerly opening it with my family I saw it was my t-shirt. I was so excited to try it on, and it was a perfect fit. The note on my package said to wear the t-shirt on our graduation Zoom tomorrow, and I was excited for the last day of school to come.

Last Day Of School

Yay! When I woke up in the morning of the last day of 5th grade, and went downstairs for breakfast, it was pancakes! My sister's and my favorite breakfast is pancakes, and my mom made it for us to make the day special. After eating the yummy pancakes, my sister and I both headed up. I had my t-shirt on, and logged into the graduation party Zoom link. All of the 5th graders at my school were there and I saw lots of my friends. The principal was also there, and after about ten minutes of waiting for more people to head in she started talking about how graduation is a big milestone, and that she was proud of all of us for working so hard even through the difficult switch. She then showed us a video celebrating each one of us with a picture, and our names with some music in the background. It was so cool to see so many of my friends and classmates.

At the end of the meeting, our teachers told all of us to check our email because they created a virtual yearbook for us. So, as soon as the Zoom ended and I said goodbye, I opened up my email and saw a google slide with my classmates' pictures, and notes they wrote for me, as well as a note written from my teacher. It was such a nice surprise, and I was so happy to read all the notes they wrote for me. It was honestly the best online graduation, and I was so happy I tried to concentrate on the positive rather than brooding over the sad things I would miss.

Over the summer every year we would go to meet our grandparents, and since last year we didn't we were so excited to go this year. But, because of COVID lockdown, we couldn't go this year either. We were all really sad because we couldn't visit our family as it was always so much fun to go. I was really annoyed that we couldn't go, but I tried to just ignore the thoughts, and try to enjoy the summer in a new way.

After about a week of summer, we got an email from the school district giving us many different resources to keep ourselves busy over the summer. I quickly scanned through and opened the links of some including Skillshare, Wave, KCLS, Teen Advisory Group, and others. I looked into some Wave classes, and signed up for some along with my sister. We signed up for Tennis, Journaling, Card Making, Photography, Junior Medical Academy and Intro to Java. I jotted down the dates for these programs so I wouldn't miss them this summer. I also checked Skillshare, and explored the different classes, and was interested to learn some dance and art from it. After looking into some of the other links I found some events to sign up for in KCLS, I looked through them and signed up for some really cool author online visits, I also signed up for some art classes.

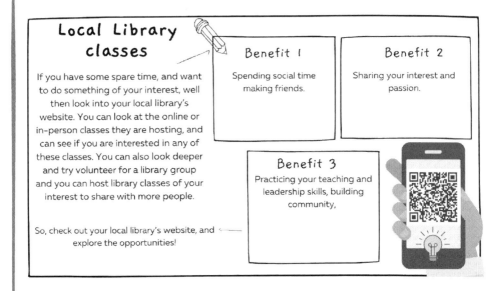

Local Library classes

If you have some spare time, and want to do something of your interest, well then look into your local library's website. You can look at the online or in-person classes they are hosting, and can see if you are interested in any of these classes. You can also look deeper and try volunteer for a library group and you can host library classes of your interest to share with more people.

So, check out your local library's website, and explore the opportunities!

Benefit 1
Spending social time making friends.

Benefit 2
Sharing your interest and passion.

Benefit 3
Practicing your teaching and leadership skills, building community,

My sister joined a volunteering group in KCLS called Teen Advisory Group, and she said you can create your own events with other members and host them for other people to attend and learn something you want to teach. She was having her first one about gift wrapping out of recycled material, and it sounded really cool. I felt bad, that I didn't sign up earlier, and asked her if she could sign me up as well. And, she was able to so we were planning on hosting some art classes together. I was so happy to be in those planning meetings. I also learned what volunteer hours were, and that doing these events counted as volunteering.

Finally, it was the week that my wave classes started. I was so hyped to learn new things, and learn more about my interests. In the morning the Junior Medical Academy class took place. At the beginning, I learned about BioEngineering, Medical Biotechnology, and, cells in the body. Some parts I didn't fully understand because they were aimed for high school students, but I understood most of it. After some time learning, people shared why they were interested in the medical field and some stories were heart-touching. When it was my turn to speak, I said that I was interested because of how many people were suffering from different things and they all need a different cure. Every day I see humans with different health problems. By being in the medical field I hope to one day help them get better. After some more people shared, the founders were talking more about the different chapters, and said we could start our own chapter where we live. I was so excited because I would love to start a chapter where I could teach and spread this amazing opportunity to learn more. They sent an email with pages and pages of things we had to read through, and a long document of how to set up a chapter, and I was super overwhelmed that I had to read all of this. My dad suggested I read a little bit each day, and so I worked on that, and the system went pretty well.

The next day my sister and I both had a KCLS class we were hosting as part of TAG. The class was about how to make a gingerbread cupcake. We hosted this class with another one of our friends, and went back and forth on camera sharing each step over Zoom. It was so fun to do, and the cupcakes tasted great at the end. I really enjoyed TAG because it was like a small community, and we could share our passion with more people by hosting events. There were some glitches with the technology, and I was quite anxious if I was saying things right, but after some time I started to really enjoy sharing the recipe, and especially eating the cupcake afterwards.

Over the weekend, my sister and I would build a fort in our living room since we had some time after our classes. We also spent some time binge watching Disney movies. It was really fun and we tried to make the most of our time together. We loved getting to spend time together and we loved doing so many different things during our sister time.

After my Junior Medical Academy class was over, I was spending some time on Skillshare exploring the different classes. I looked at some of the classes like Karate moves, and hip- hop steps. They were well explained and easy to follow along. I looked around even more for different classes.

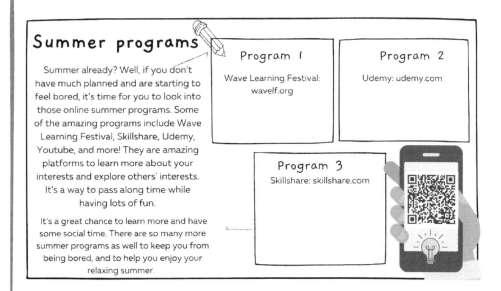

As I was doing this, I came across a bullet journaling video make by Amanda Rach Lee. It was really cool to see such neatness and organization. I showed my sister her classes as well, and she loved them. As I watched some of her other classes with my sister, in one of the classes she said that there are so many different ways to use your bullet journal, and you can use it in any way that will help you the most.

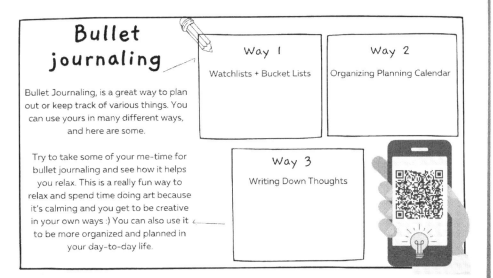

Bullet journaling

Bullet Journaling, is a great way to plan out or keep track of various things. You can use yours in many different ways, and here are some.

Try to take some of your me-time for bullet journaling and see how it helps you relax. This is a really fun way to relax and spend time doing art because it's calming and you get to be creative in your own ways :) You can also use it to be more organized and planned in your day-to-day life.

Way 1

Watchlists + Bucket Lists

Way 2

Organizing Planning Calendar

Way 3

Writing Down Thoughts

This got me to start thinking about how over the summer I could make one of my notebooks into my own bullet journal. I told my sister and she loved the idea, so both of us started searching for a journal we hadn't used yet. As soon as we found one, we each started brainstorming what we would use our bullet journals for. I decided to use my bullet journal for writing down my thoughts and doodling because I can always look back to my journal and see what I thought before. Also, doodling is always so fun, and nice to see what comes. My sister decided to use her bullet journal to plan her schedules and classes. After that day, I used to spend 10-20 minutes daily just writing in my journal about my thoughts about summer and my art ideas. This really helped me to release those feelings and thoughts in a creative way. I love spending my me time doing this because it's really nice to have it all written down instead of floating around in my head.

Story Writing

During the week I had attended a couple online author visits from KCLS that I signed up for earlier. Some of the authors I met virtually included Vera Brosgol, Gale Galligan, and Katherine Sparrow, some very famous authors. The authors shared their stories, and what made them want to become authors. Their stories really inspired me because of how they tried to include some of their life details into their books. After listening to the authors share about how amazing the process can be, and saying some of the difficulties in writing, but also some of the benefits. I started thinking about what Emma Shevah said to me during her school visit. I remember she said for an aspiring author you can start by writing short stories to get your creative flow. When I asked those three authors the same questions, they said the same things, to start now by writing creative pieces. So, I set a goal to write some different stories over the summer.

I sat down that evening, opened up a google document and started thinking of a fictional story line. I started by creating a mind map for my book. And, after I had some characters created, and a plot, I decided to start typing and see where the story would go. After some time, I took a pause and decided I would return to this tomorrow with some new thoughts. Just before dinner, I told my family what I was doing, and how it felt really good to write.

They asked me if I remembered the amount of short story books I had created when I was younger, and I still did. Immediately, my sister and I ran upstairs and looked in my keepsake box of things I had brought from Ireland, and found my old story books. We both read through it and laughed about the different stories I wrote because they made no sense whatsoever. But it was really nice to see that I always loved writing, and it made me think of actually being an author one day.

Mind maps

Are u planning on writing a story, an essay, taking notes, or studying for an exam? Well, then your must have trick is using a mind map. Well, what is a mind map? A mind map involves writing down a main theme and thinking of new and related ideas which expand out from the centre which connect.

Mind maps are really helpful, and they can be used in multiple different ways to help with your different needs. Be sure to look into them and research more about how to use them and experiment with them if you ever find the need!

Benefit 1
Find better solutions fast.

Benefit 2
Help you collect more information

Benefit 3
More effective collaboration method, and it definitely increases productivity.

Some of the stories I wrote were about unicorns, burgers, and also an island. After spending some time re-reading my book, and working with my mom (an author) to check the plot and do some editing, I decided to leave the story like it was for now. I was proud of what I did. Even though I could have added some more things to it, I wanted to start a new story. I already had an idea in mind for my other story, I wanted it to be about a boy who is in a wheelchair, and how he went about finding friends in his new school. As I was writing, I enjoyed adding details to the character and making the character

The Wheelchair

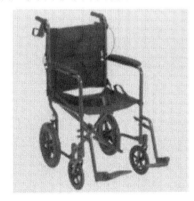

have some traits that I observed in different people. Also, when I was stuck, I would imagine being there with the character, and tried to imagine the millions of possibilities that could happen next. I really enjoyed building the story, and being creative with the details.

After our wave classes were over for the day, we had spare time, and I wanted to do some sports for fun. So, my sister, dad, and I decided to play tennis in the evening. I was so excited to take what I was learning about tennis in the wave class, and actually apply it when playing. And since my sister was doing tennis classes from a coach, she knew more about it and could teach me. We started by doing a warm-up. My sister then practiced some shots we learned in the wave class. It was so much fun, and our dad even challenged my sister and me to do 20 shots back and forth, and finally when we overcame the challenge, we all headed home. It was really fun to spend time with my dad and sister, as well as doing some sports. We wanted to do this every evening.

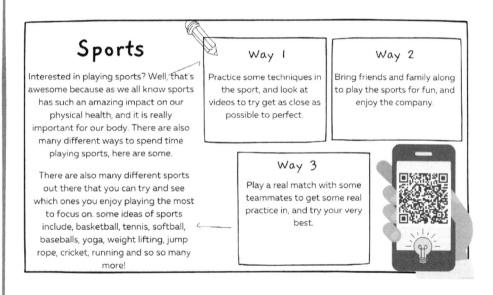

The next day, in the evening when we were just heading out to go play tennis, I wanted to bring my basketball since there is a basketball court right next to the tennis courts, and if there was time, I thought we could play. So, when we drove up to the tennis courts, we all decided to play some basketball and then tennis. We tried to shoot some hoops, one at a time. After some time playing basketball, we played some tennis, and then headed home.

The next day, my dad said he wasn't going to be able to make it in the evening to play tennis and basketball because he had an office meeting at the same time, but he said that my sister and I could check in with our friends to see if they were free to play. So, I texted my friend to see if she was free to play basketball. And my sister texted her friend who lives in our neighborhood as well to see if she could play tennis.

When, they both replied saying the evening would work perfectly to play. We all walked started walking to the school where the basketball and tennis courts were.

My sister and her friend went to play tennis, while my friend and I played basketball. My friend taught me some rules in the game, and also some basketball practice games, which we started playing. It was so fun to play basketball with her because she taught me so well and we also chatted about how summer was going. After that, we all headed back to our houses, and decided to play like this more often. We created a group chat to plan when we would meet up next to play.

The weekend arrived! Saturday, we all went to a beach, and played in the water, we also made pizza for lunch. On Sunday, my sister and I said we had something special for them in the evening. They were excited for what it was and we were trying to keep the secret. During the day, we decided to go veggie picking at our local farm, Baileys. We picked out some corn, cabbage, zucchini, cucumber and potato. After some time, we headed back home. We wanted to eat outside for lunch, but due to COVID all shops were only delivery. So, we made a panini for lunch, and watched TV while eating it. Then we asked our parents to go upstairs for an hour and half so we could make our surprise.

Dinner Night

Our surprise was a dinner night for both of them. We both created a restaurant name, "Café D 'More," and also made a ticket for them. We prepared all the food including pasta, garlic bread, and also a small lava cake we made.

Finally, it was all set and ready for them to come down and enjoy the food. We told them to change into some nice clothes. We then walked them downstairs. Just after coming down the stairs, the disco lights we plugged in created a really nice ambiance and made the seating look more professional and surprising. Then, we brought all the food and took a seat at the table; they seemed very impressed with the presentation and taste. We were so happy they enjoyed it. After the most delicious dessert we took pictures. My parents thanked us, and said they loved this dinner and it was so special to them. This made my sister and me feel so happy, because we love doing family nights like this. It felt good to share our gratitude for everything they do for us through a dinner night because it's creative and we knew they would love it. They also said that we should wait because they would make us a dinner night in the coming future as well.

The week after, our wave classes came to an end, and so my sister and I wanted to do something else to keep ourselves busy. We decided to create a mini art shack like we saw in Andi Mack. We decided to create an indoor art shack in our guest room since there was lots of space after taking out the bed. We asked our dad for help during the week. To start off, we went to the garage and found some boards to create the structure, we also brought a drill and some screws. We started building the shack, and after about 2-3 days of hard work and planning, it was complete. Now, it was time for my sister and I to start making it look good, and organizing all of our supplies. We needed a table, and decided to buy one when we went to Ikea in a couple of weeks. As a temporary table, my sister got a box, wrapped it with tape and put a tablecloth around it, and it was perfect. It looked so beautiful, and was just what we wanted.

Sister Spa

I really enjoy spending time with my sister, and am so grateful to have her. I wanted to show her how much she means to me, and wanted to surprise her, so, I started to brainstorm surprises I could give her. After a while, I thought of an awesome one - a sister spa night. For this, I had an idea of creating an Orbeez foot massage. I planned to have the spa night on Thursday. Since I had more than a week, I decided to start planning ahead. I wrote a reminder for myself that on Tuesday, I would soak the dried Orbeez in water so they could grow and be ready for the spa day. Then, I wrote down all the tasks I needed to get ready.

Surprise Sister Night

Agenda

* 4 - 5 → Spa
* 5 - 5:30 → Dessert
* 5:30 - 7 → Movie

Preparation

Print the flyer

1. Get Aloe vera facial masks ready, get hair combs gathered, and get orbeez for the footbath.
   - Cut a cucumber for the eyes, a onesie, and a headband. A warm, moist towel for the head. Get relaxing music.
2. Get a fro-yo toppings bar ready, with ice cream or yogurt.
3. Get the set up for disney+ tv ready, and get cozy.

The day of the spa finally arrived! I told my sister to sit in her room for one hour so I could get the surprise ready. During that hour, I set up the table, face masks, the Orbeez box, some moist towels, and I set up a movie on my computer to watch after.

I printed out a flyer so she could see the plan. After an hour or so, I handed her the flyer. She was super happy, and gave me a big hug. It was the best feeling. First we went to the kitchen to make frozen yogurt. We took out toppings and made our delicious treat. We ate some, and then headed to the spa area. We put the face mask on, while watching TV and then stuck our feet into the Orbeez box (which she really liked), while watching TV. Next, we took pictures, and relaxed in the bed. It was so nice and she was very impressed, and enjoyed spending time with me. It was nice to just spend time together, trying out a new "night." It's so cool to know there are many ways to spend time with my sister, and that we could create new events or things to do together.

Website

It was already August, and there was just over a month left until school started. I was super excited for the last month of summer. I wanted to do something inspiring and positive because during such crazy times, it's not just me experiencing boredom and missing out on social time. I talked to my family, and my dad suggested creating a website. I thought that was a great idea, and my sister was doing a website for baking tips and recipes. I was thinking of what the website could be about and thought it should have blog posts. I was thinking of a logo and name, and while I was just doodling one day, my dad said the character I was creating looked like a titbit yogi, and I thought that was a great idea for a website name. So, I called it Titbit Yogi and wanted to post little blogs and call them titbits. My dad and I sat down and started to create a promotional video, a catchphrase, and chose photos, and edited everything together with some background music. The website was ready to launch and I decided to post every other day.

When we weren't working on our websites, my sister and I did some journaling. We also watched YouTube videos from the channel "I Draw, You Cook." We both loved watching the videos for different reasons. I enjoyed watching because I liked seeing how creative the cooks were, and my sister loved the ingredients they made dishes with. While watching, we both had the best idea, we wanted to do our own round of "I Draw, You Cook." So, for lunch the next day, we asked our parents to draw something random, and we told them that we would try to make it out of food. My sister and I decided to make different dishes, and see whose looked more like what my parents drew. She made two plates, and I made two plates. After drawing out our plans, we started putting things together on the plate, and then it was time for lunch. We called them over, and showed them our creations compared to their drawings. They were amazed by how well we had recreated the drawings. The food was also yummy. It was so fun to cook in a creative way like that. I definitely wanted to do it again.

During the weekend, our parents said they had a surprise for us. They told us to stay upstairs for one hour in the evening. Then they surprised us with a dinner night. It was so fun because they were all dressed up like chefs, and we both wore dresses as instructed. They served us loaded enchiladas, and for dessert they gave us a rose made from chocolate. After finishing the deliciously cheesy food and awesome chocolate, we took pictures. It was so nice to see how different they made their restaurant. My sister and I loved the surprise and felt very special.

Since there were now only two weeks of summer left, we received an email about the next school year of 2020-2021. The superintendent shared that due to COVID, they would have to continue school online for now. I was super super super upset after hearing this because I was looking forward to my first year of middle school in-person because we would get lockers, and I could attend clubs. I was also looking forward to the in-person experience. My sister was also really upset because she wanted to have an in-person last year of middle school. We both wanted to see each other in school since we would both be in middle school... the online experience is so different.

I was still really nervous about middle school because I wasn't sure how hard it would be, and whether it was difficult to get full credit. When I was biking with my sister, I asked her how hard middle school was and she said that if you try your best and work hard, then you'll get a great grade. I was still nervous and anxious about this but talking to her helped me a bit.

A couple of days later, my school emailed saying to get textbooks and elective kits, come by during the afternoon and collect them at curbside pickup. I was really excited to get my textbooks, and my pre-tech kit. My sister was also excited to get her things. I was still upset there wasn't going to be a jumpstart day, because jumpstart days always sound so cool, since you get to open lockers in middle school, say hi to teachers, and get your school photo. I felt really sad that I was going to miss that amazing experience.

After collecting our textbooks, my sister said hello to some of the staff she knew, and also the librarian through the car window. After driving home, my sister and I organized all of our school supplies, and the textbooks we bought earlier. After organizing and cleaning up our rooms, we both set up our desks for online learning.

It was the last week of summer, and my sister and I tried to spend a lot of time together since we wouldn't spend too much time together once school started. We spent time in the pool and also did some website blogging. It was really fun, but I was still having some anxiousness, and during the night I couldn't sleep because I was so nervous about starting middle school. This usually happens when I am overthinking. So, like always I tried to do some belly breathing exercises which helped me to fall asleep faster. I decided to write down my thoughts about middle school in a journal, so I could get it on paper and make it easier to see. I took some time to understand what thoughts were circulating through my head about school, and write them down. After doing this, I felt much lighter and more energetic. Writing in my bullet journal really helps me to connect with myself, and accept all my thoughts.

As a family, we always prioritized spending time together because we know how important it is, especially when things are hard for each other. So, my mom suggested that we all say three nice things about each other because it seemed that we were all a little upset about the schooling change, and so we could be more uplifted. First, we all said nice things about my mom, like the way she prioritizes us, spends time with us, how understanding she is, and also she gives really nice big hugs. It was really cool to see that we said similar things.

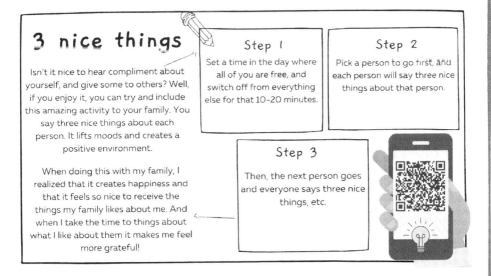

3 nice things

Isn't it nice to hear compliment about yourself, and give some to others? Well, if you enjoy it, you can try and include this amazing activity to your family. You say three nice things about each person. It lifts moods and creates a positive environment.

When doing this with my family, I realized that it creates happiness and that it feels so nice to receive the things my family likes about me. And when I take the time to things about what I like about them it makes me feel more grateful!

Step 1
Set a time in the day where all of you are free, and switch off from everything else for that 10-20 minutes.

Step 2
Pick a person to go first, and each person will say three nice things about that person.

Step 3
Then, the next person goes and everyone says three nice things, etc.

Next, we all said nice things about my dad. We said that we liked the way he's so supportive; we like how he always helps us; and we also like the way he always asks us about how we're feeling. Then, we all said three things that we really liked about my sister. I said I really like the way she always talks to me and I can talk to her openly. I like the way she prioritizes spending time with me and the way she shows unconditional love to us all. Last but definitely not least, we talked about me. Everyone said the things they liked about me and they said how I always bring positive vibes into the house, how I'm always bubbly and make others happy and that I do things to bring the family together like arrange movie nights, game nights and other things like that.

I enjoyed having this short, meaningful conversation, because it felt nice to say the things we liked about each other, and it was also nice to hear things that others liked. It felt great to spend time appreciating others, because sometimes we get carried away and don't take time to do these important things. It was a nice distraction from everything on my mind, and I felt more energized after. And doing this activity on regular basis helps us to give praises and receives praises too.

Middle School

Finally, my first day of middle school arrived. After breakfast, I headed upstairs to my room, and logged into my homeroom meeting. Then, I logged into the 6th graders virtual welcome assembly. Later that day, I joined the WEB small group activity meeting, where WEB leaders (some 8th graders) played virtual games with us and made us feel comfortable. It was really fun, and my sister was also a WEB leader. We were assigned WEB leaders as well and did some introduction games with them. Even though it was online, they made it really fun. After that, we all logged off, and our first day of school was over, though it was a half day.

It took a couple of weeks getting used to school and the new online learning platform, Schoology. Remembering the order of all my classes was a bit confusing as well. Every day I would look forward to Band class, because it was one of the only classes where I knew the people and had connections with them. And, since we all started learning our instruments together in 5th grade band last year, it was so cool to resume our community. It was so fun to learn more about my instrument, but super weird doing it online for the first couple days of figuring out how to make the most of online learning for band.

During morning slides, we usually get some updates in the school, and this time there was an announcement for all interested 6th graders to apply for Associated Student Body (ASB). In the slide there was some information about what ASB is, and how to apply. I was really interested in applying because it was a leadership role, and you get to work with your peers and make school a fun environment. I wasn't sure if I would get in, and if I would be able to make time for this as it's a pretty big leadership role, but I decided that I would try my best, as it was one of my interests. To be part of ASB, there was an interest form, then an informational meeting, then an application Google form, and lastly if you get through that step, there is a speech you need to record and share with the whole 6th grade for them to view and vote. So, as per the first step, I filled out the interest form after telling my family about this awesome opportunity.

During the week, I got an email from ASB, giving the Zoom link to the informational meeting. When I logged into the meeting that day there were 7th and 8th grade ASB members presenting about ASB, and sharing what projects we get to work on. After the meeting, they gave us the application form to fill out. The Google form appeared to be very long, and just looking through it I started to get overwhelmed and unsure about how to fill it in before the deadline. I took a couple of deep breaths, and decided to divide the questions into doable bits. I planned on doing it over five days, and answer two questions daily.

Filling out a form

Are you interested in applying for some programs, and there's a long form that's required to fill out to be part of the program? Well, that's something we all have to deal with sometime. So, here's a tip that can help you to fill out the form, and now be overwhelmed.

Before you know it the form is submitted, and you put in all the required information! You can finally relax, and let the pressure of filling out hte form fade away. By the way, Congratulations, and good luck!

Step 1
First look through and count how many questions there are, and the due date.

Step 2
Divide it over the span of a couple days, and each day do some 4-5 questions.

Step 3
After you complete filling out roughly the questions, and have 1-2 days before you need to submit it, be sure to check the form over and add some more sentences and check the spelling and grammar.

By the end of the week, I completed all the questions, looked over my answers, and asked my dad to help double check as well. Finally, I could submit the form, and feel the relief.

After calming down from the freak out session, I thought about how the other ASB candidates were dealing with this, and thought they would be doing fine, so I should just go for it like them, and be pleased with whatever the outcome is. So, feeling calmer, I started to type out a speech, and looked at a couple of examples online to get more ideas. After some brainstorming and planning, I was ready to record my speech. It took a couple of tries, and some patience from my dad and sister recording, but finally my speech was ready to submit. Thought I did hesitate before clicking, my sister convinced me to go for it, and said she would be proud of me no matter what.

That week during history, there was a slide with the link to all 6th grade candidates' videos. It was time for the teacher to at last click my video, so I decided to turn off my camera, and just breath in and out and hoped for the best. And, before I knew it, my video was over, and the next one started playing. After viewing all the videos, everyone including the candidates, filled out a Google form with four candidates they thought would be good for ASB.

The next week, I got an email for ASB with the results of whose in ASB. I didn't want to open, because I was really anxious if I got in or not, just like when I get a result on my test, I don't want to open it immediately because I don't want to know what score I got.

But after getting the nerve to open it with my family, the email read "Congratulations, you got into 2020-21 ASB." I was super hyped after reading the email! The email also contained information about future meetings for ASB. I felt so happy to get in to ASB, and was so grateful for the opportunity. I was also relived that putting myself out there didn't have such a bad impact I had presumed it would. I hoped that everyone who wasn't able to make it was okay, and knew that they did a great job by putting themselves out there, and being brave.

My sister also got into ASB. Her ASB application process had been at the end of last school year since she was now in 8th grade. So, now both of us were in ASB. During our later meetings we both sometimes recorded morning announcements together, and we also took part in the siblings' morning announcement segment. Recording the segment was really fun, because there was a mini trivia and the other students who watched the announcements said they loved it.

Think Positive Club

My sister loves aviation, and wants to become an astronaut, and has many opportunities for flying. She wanted to share the passion with more youth, to do this, so she started a club in our school, "Sky Riders" for youth interested in aviation, aerospace and aeronautics.

This got me thinking about starting my own club. After talking to my family, I had the idea to create a club for positive thinking, and to get guest speakers for motivation. I wanted this club to be for everyone, as a fun and relaxing place, but also filled with lots of excitement and activities. I thought it was most needed during these times where we can't talk in person, so this club would be a place to chat and be there for each other. I also wanted it to be really fun, and for everyone to have a good time as well as learn some tips along their journey.

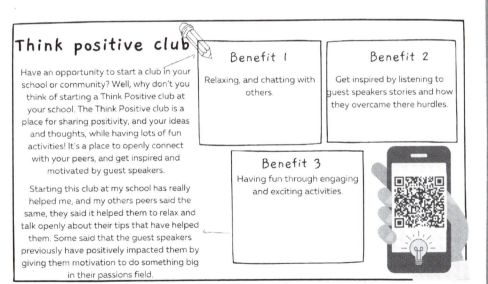

Think positive club

Have an opportunity to start a club in your school or community? Well, why don't you think of starting a Think Positive club at your school. The Think Positive club is a place for sharing positivity, and your ideas and thoughts, while having lots of fun activities! It's a place to openly connect with your peers, and get inspired and motivated by guest speakers.

Starting this club at my school has really helped me, and my others peers said the same, they said it helped them to relax and talk openly about their tips that have helped them. Some said that the guest speakers previously have positively impacted them by giving them motivation to do something big in their passions field.

Benefit 1
Relaxing, and chatting with others.

Benefit 2
Get inspired by listening to guest speakers stories and how they overcame there hurdles.

Benefit 3
Having fun through engaging and exciting activities.

I talked to my sister about the process of starting a club at school and she told me about creating a club constitution and getting approval from ASB. After filling out some forms, and getting an awesome supervisor, and some kids interested, I was able to get my club approved from my ASB peers and advisors. I was so happy that the "Think Positive" club was up and running.

For our first meeting, I presented a slideshow and talked about what the club was and the things we were planning in the near future and that we would be having many guest speakers. For our first meeting, we had at least 15 members attend.

I decided to talk to my mom and ask her to be a guest speaker and talk about mindfulness, since she is a mindfulness teacher. She gave me other contacts for guest speakers who would talk on topics like mental health, inspiration, time management, and gratitude. I contacted all of them to set a time for them to come and talk if they were interested. During our next club meeting, before the guest speaker came, we talked about our lives, interests, and also shared different tips we use to go through life. I felt like these conversations were very uplifting and also everyone showed empathy and compassion which made the club feel like a safe place for all.

Being in this club, helped me to calm down after a long day of online school, and was a happy environment where I felt comfortable sharing my tips and acting on other people's tips. It was my happy place, and many of the others who joined said they felt comfortable sharing in the group and that the guest speakers really helped them with tips to use in their daily lives. I was so glad the club was helping so many people and that we were creating a small community. The club supervisor, was a counselor and she helped so much in sharing activities, and also with getting the club promoted in the morning announcements.

After school one day, when I was scrolling through YouTube looking for some positive videos to show the club, I came across the YouTube channel, Kid President. I clicked onto one of his videos "Kid President's 25 Reasons To Be

Thankful!" After watching this video, I felt like I should be more grateful about everything I have, and this video articulated very well that you can be thankful for almost anything. So, I decided to show this video in one of the club meetings, and everyone loved it and said how they want to start being more thankful for what they have.

After school, I made time to attend KCLS library events online and to host them. My sister and I attended a KCLS event called "Save Lives with STEM." During the event, we learned about the spread of malaria, and learned how scientists and researchers are trying to reduce the spread with different technology. It was really interesting, and I learned a lot about this disease, and I wanted to learn more about it as well. It was nice to spend time to attend this event because I learned lots and it's also another way to socialize.

My sister and I hosted a bullet journaling series through TAG, where we showed some skills we had learned from the WAVE classes we attended, and YouTube videos, as well as our own experiments and creations. There were a lot of attendees, almost 30+ who logged into the Zoom. So many people were showing their creations. It was lots of fun to see everyone's creations, and to show my own creation at the same time. Hosting these classes was so much fun because everyone unmuted and we had conversations about YouTube channels we would recommend, and everyone shared more and more that we all wanted to see. It was like a little art community with every event we did, and it felt nice to do art but also teach others some ideas to express themselves creatively.

After our last event of the bullet journaling series, the TAG advisor told us about the Presidential Volunteer Service Award. She shared the website link, and told us to check the amount of volunteer hours we earned from TAG, and how many hours you need to apply for the award. After checking, we had just enough hours to earn the gold pin, so we filled out the form given by the advisor, and she told us that in March we would receive a package including a gold pin, certificate, and a letter signed by the President of the United States. I was super excited, and was glad the application process was so simple. It is so cool that just volunteering for fun, and being motivated by helping the community can give such an awesome package.

After school one day, my mom showed me some books to see if club members would be interested in them. I picked out the two most colorful books. The titles read "Just Feel" and "Just Breathe," from the "Just Be" series by Mallika Chopra.

After reading the first couple of pages in both books I wanted to try out some of the activities. Since there were lots of really cool ones I decided that every night before bed I would do one of the activities. As I was doing the activities daily, I realized they really helped me to ground before bed. I also noticed that the activities helped me to have more control over my breathing.

Some of the activities also helped me to be more aware of my surroundings and be more in the present moment. Even though it was hard to spend time reading the books, without fidgeting or doing movement activities. The engaging pictures and the fonts of the book helped me to concentrate more, and I was able to read the book more easily.

After a couple of days of reading and experimenting with the calming activities, I thought it may really benefit the club members in Think Positive. So, I shared these two amazing books, and they all loved reading the samples. As a club, we all started to do the books' activities during our weekly online meetings.

It was already November, and we were two months into the school year. Gradually I started getting more homework and also more projects. In science we were learning about density and matter. In history we were learning about civilizations and ancient writings. In math we were learning about dividing fractions, and how to solve functions. In English we were doing weekly 20-word vocabulary quizzes, and in fitness we were doing online workout videos. In band class, we used smart music to play sheet music; our band teacher still made online learning really fun hosting Kahoots and giving us fun assignments. Through these hectic times, I still maintained my habit of using a to do list which made it easier to work.

Because winter break was coming up, the teachers pushed a lot more work on us, and I started to feel overwhelmed. So in our weekly Think Positive club meeting, we discussed ways to keep pushing through and how we could be less overwhelmed. Perfectly in tune, our guest speaker, Erin Jones, shared tips for how to stay positive, how to get inspired, and she also shared about her life story, and how she became a motivational speaker. Everyone loved her, and I loved the way she said to share your talent with the world, and to help others with your talent.

Suddenly, there were only two weeks till winter break, and we were all really excited to have a chance to relax after so much online learning, and being restrained in our seats all day looking at the computer.

One evening, we started to decorate the Christmas tree we bought. We had a plastic Christmas tree in Ireland, but when we came here, my sister had an idea to get a live Christmas tree so we could keep it alive and reuse it ever year. After decorating it, we loved how special and brightened up the house looked.

Winter Break

It was finally winter break and snow was falling like crazy. My sister and I love to sled down the small slope in our backyard and on the roads in our neighborhood. We tried to build a snowman in our backyard and did some mega snowball fights. When we started to freeze, we would go inside and change into our comfiest PJ's and have some Irish hot chocolate, while watching the best, most iconic Christmas movies. It was so nice to spend time with my family like that, and to know that there was no school and it was just my time to relax and enjoy myself.

For our end of the year ritual, my mom proposed an idea to add to our gratitude jar. She said that we could also write down three things we accomplished over the year, and three goals for the next year. We all loved the idea, to reflect how the year had gone and look into the next year, and decided this would be our new ritual. This got me super excited for Christmas Eve to come so we could do our rituals.

Setting goals

Having trouble completing something? Well, setting goals can help you persevere till you achieve your goal, and when there is something exciting as a treat when you finish, it makes wanting to reach the goal even stronger.

Setting goals is very helpful, and setting S.M.A.R.T.(specific, measurable, achievable, relevant, and time-bound.) goals makethem easier to reach. When you complete your goal, and get a treator celebration then, you can follow these steps again for another goal!

Step 1
Think of tasks that are hard for you to do because you have no interest.

Step 2
Think of a goal that would help you want to complete the task, like, finishing my reading assignment and get a 90% or above.

Step 3
Once you do step 1 and 2, know it's time for you to decide on a treat you give yourself for completing the goal as a driving force, like a candy, food, or maybe a break if there is one coming up.

Finally, it was time to start our rituals, after reading through all of our gratitude jar notes we wrote throughout the year. We wrote three things we accomplished over the year of 2020, then we wrote three goals we had for 2021. After we all finished writing down our ideas, we read what we had written, and expanded on what we wrote. It was so interesting to hear what my mom, dad and sister wrote, and it was nice to share what I wrote down.

For the next couple of days, we binged movies, played in the snow, and baked and cooked.

At last, it was New Year's Eve, the last day of the year. I was super excited. I felt like doing something really fun as a family, so I looked up some ideas in the morning for what we could do. I scrolled through and found some really cool family game night ideas, like minute to win it challenges and others games. I wrote down the games I wanted to try, and all the items we need to set up the games. After my sister woke up, I told her my plan and she loved the idea and said she would love to help set up and also make some snacks.

After we all had some delicious noodles for lunch, we told my parents to go upstairs, so we could set up the family game night and snack bar. After some hard work finding all the things around the house, and moving the sofas to the side to make some space for the table to display the snack bar and some space for the games, we were ready to begin the Family Game Night! Once they came down, I explained how to play the games. Then my sister talked about the snacks she had prepared. After eating some snacks, we started to play the minute to win it challenges, and used the timer, it was super exciting. Then, we played some other games like mini bowling.

The night filled with games and snacks was nearly over, and it was time for us to do the ten second countdown till the new year came. We all counted down, 10, 9... while watching fireworks exploding in the sky a distance from our house. It was great to be with my family celebrating another year of our lives together!

Conclusion

This is my journey, starting from the move from Ireland to US, adjusting to the new norm, suddenly hit by COVID, and finally coping with social distancing. You may have connected to some of the experiences that I experienced, and you may have gone through them differently. You may have also experienced many of the same emotions and feelings I did and still do go through, but I hope after reading this book that you will have some tips and techniques to deal with whatever unexpected things life throws at you. These tips are just some of the many ideas out there. If you like any tips, be sure to highlight them and add them to your tool kit for any time you need them, you can also write them down somewhere you will always see. You can test some out and see if they help you out. If you like these tips, be sure to share with others and tag me on Instagram @taanvis_inspiration

Every human being is gifted with talent and a purpose. It's your mission to figure out your talent and use it to fulfill your purpose. Your journey is not a road without bumps, but hopefully these tips will help to ensure that you overcome the bumps as smoothly and safely as possible. This is just the beginning. There are so many other emotions and experiences people go through, so I would recommend you explore other resources. I have added a few that helped me in the resources section. Just remember, you are capable, you are talented, and you are SUPERCALIFRAGILISTICEXPIALIDOCIOUS!

Want to read more? Be sure to stay tuned for more of the story by following me on Instagram @taanvis.inspiration :)
Youtube @Uplift Teens Today
Blog @taanvi.us

Resources

Websites:

- ➤ nami.org
- ➤ nami-eastside.org
- ➤ cope2thrive.com
- ➤ namiwa.org

Youtube:

- ➤ **Breathing Techniques**
    - o Headspace
    - o The Mental Health Teacher
- ➤ **Expressing:**
    - o MGHClayCenter
- ➤ **Mental Health**
    - o NAMI
    - o The Live Love Laugh Foundation
- ➤ **Motivational & Pep Talks**
    - o Participant Kid President
    - o TED
    - o TEDx Talks
    - o TEDxYouth
- ➤ **Quick Mindfulness**
    - o The Mental Health Teacher
    - o Headspace
    - o Creative Mindfulness
- ➤ **Social Media**
    - o Common Sense Education

Books:

➢ Chopra, Mallika. Just Breathe. New York, Running Press Kids, August 28, 2018.

➢ Chopra, Mallika. Just Feel. New York, Running Press Kids, October 22, 2019.

➢ Chopra, Mallika. Just Be You. New York, Running Press Kids, March 2, 2021.

➢ Letran, Jacqui. I would, but my DAMN MIND won't let me! Dunedin, A Healed Mind, September 29, 2016

➢ Covey, Sean. The 7 Habits of Highly Effective Teens. New York, Simon & Schuster, Inc., May 27, 2014.

➢ Katragadda, Srimanju. Connect to Your Inner Guide. Vancouver, Hay House India, November 1, 2016.

➢ Taylor L. Richard, Jr. 31 Days of Power. January 21, 2021

Index

Where to find what tip box (lightbulbs)?

TAANVI AREKAPUDI

Uplift Teens Today

ABOUT ME

Taanvi Arekapudi is a 13-year-old Irish teenager with Indian parents. She is currently a student in the Northshore School District in Washington and a recipient of **C.P. and Dorothy Johnson Humanitarian Award for the year 2022**. She is an amazing leader, humanitarian, and change maker. She has also received the **Presidential Volunteer Service Award** for volunteering over 350 hours in a year through her library, school, clubs, aviation program, and homeless shelter.

She is the creator and **president of the Empowering Teens** group at her school, which she founded at the age of 12 years old. Her goal was to create a place for youth to open up, connect and learn skills that would help cope with their mental health in a fun and loving environment. Her ability to lead her peers by example toward the very best versions of themselves is exceptional. She always practices great kindness and is the embodiment of curiosity and the pursuit of knowledge. She is a **Youth Ambassador for NAMI Eastside**, East King County Affiliate of the National Alliance on Mental Illness supporting families, friends, and individuals living with mental health conditions.

CONTACT ME

www.taanvi.us   info@taanvi.us

Made in the USA
Columbia, SC
18 October 2022

69707157R00078